How To Change Your Sex

A Light♥hearted Look at the Hardest Thing You'll Ever Do

Lannie Rose

— LuLu Press —

To Jamie Faye Fenton,

The best friend a little t-girl ever had!

LEGAL DISCLAIMER: Information in this book is provided for informational purposes only and is not a substitute for professional medical or legal advice. You should not use the information herin for diagnosing or treating any medical, psychiatric, or health condition. If you have or suspect you have a medical problem, promptly contact your professional healthcare provider. Neither the author nor the publisher will be liable for any damages or harm that may result from any decision made or action taken in reliance on the information in this book.

First Lulu edition October 4, 2004

HOW TO CHANGE YOUR SEX: A LIGHTHEARTED LOOK AT THE HARDEST THING YOU'LL EVER DO. Copyright © 2004 by Lannie Rose. All rights reserved. No part of this publication can be reproduced, stored in a retrieval system, or transmitted in any form or by any means, electronic, mechanical, photocopying, recording or otherwise, without the prior permission of the publishers and/or authors.

While every precaution has been taken in the preparation of this book, the publisher assumes no responsibilities for errors or omissions, or for damages resulting from the use of information contained herein.

Acknowledgments

Thanks and love to all those who supported me in my transition, especially my great friend, über gender nerd Jamie Faye Fenton; the irrepressible Dish, who embodies the concept of unconditional love; Annemarie, who plowed the furrow just ahead of me; Jennifer, who showed me what a trans woman can be; and Renee Satin, who brought me out in so many ways; also to my professional team: Dr. Robert Brink, Dr. Annette Cholon, Charle Dewitt, Denaë Doyle, Adrianne Gowen, Dr. Joy Shaffer, and, most of all, Cynthia Young. Special thanks for the encouragement and many valuable suggestions from the trans women who reviewed this manuscript: Jamie Faye, Melinda, and Crissie; and especially Tori, who made invaluable contributions to the section on spouses and children. Thanks also to all the girls in the transgender discussion forums, groups, and clubs whose stories and advice I've shamelessly cadged. Finally, much love to my family—may they one day come to appreciate the wonderful gift God sent them when I was born transsexual.

Contents

Introduction 1

1 Are you transsexual? 5

2 Getting started: Dressing and going out 15

3 Sex, Part 1 39

4 Your spouse and children 53

5 Getting healthy 77

6 Therapy 85

7 Hormones 97

8 Transition 105

9 Sex Reassignment Surgery 129

10 Sex, Part 2 153

11 Starting a new life 165

   A Light♥hearted* Glossary of Terms 177

   Further reading 189

   Index 197

   About the author 205

Introduction

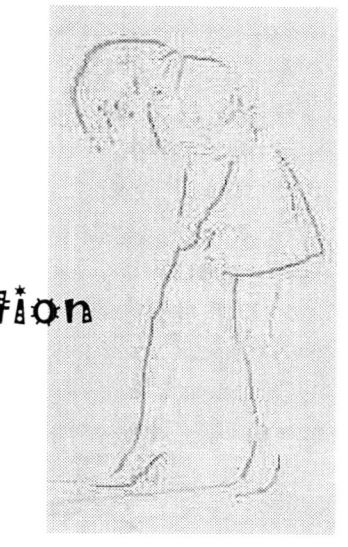

So you want to change your sex? It's a good idea—if you happen to have been born transsexual; that is, if the sex between your legs doesn't match the gender in your heart. I was born transsexual but I didn't realize it until I was 46 years old. That was just a few years ago. Then, after living my whole life up until that time as a man, I changed my sex; now I live as a woman. You can, too!

Changing your sex is not just a surgical procedure; in fact, the surgery is completely optional. What changing your sex does entail is simply changing your entire perception of your own self; and, changing your gender presentation—how you dress, how you walk and talk, how you relate to all the other people in your life, how you engage in sexual activity, your name, and all of your identification documents. You may even change what you are doing with your life.

You will probably change your body, at least in terms of your hairstyle, grooming habits (facial hair and the length of your fingernails), and ornamentation (piercings and tattoos). You will probably use hormones to make even more fundamental changes to your body. You may opt for various plastic surgeries like rhinoplasty and liposuction to further modify the appearance of your face and body. Ultimately, you may choose to change your genitals with *the operation* (as in, "Have you had *the operation?*"): sex reassignment surgery or SRS. Or, you may decide that your genitals are fine just the way they are.

There are plenty of books and other resources that discuss all aspects of transgenderism, transsexualism, and sex changes in great detail. Many of them are very good, and they contain all sorts of important information that you will probably want to know eventually. These resources tend to be long, detailed, and serious. This book, *How To Change Your Sex,* is a quick, practical, and entertaining overview of the subject. It is guide to the things you will want to learn more about. I skip over the details that you will quickly uncover as you research any of these topics further. I concentrate on the most important points and on practical advice based on my own experience and that of many other transsexual women and men I have spoken with. While I've tried to write in a lighthearted style, all of the information in this book is as accurate as I can make it and as serious as can be. Changing your sex is no joke! This book is a great starting point for someone who is just beginning to realize they have gender issues and wondering if they might eventually lead to a sex change. It's also a good overview to help family, friends, and coworkers of transsexual individuals understand the process that their loved ones may undergo.

You can change your sex from male to female (MTF) or from female to male (FTM), depending on your starting point. You can even change back again—but if you follow the advice in this book, you should never have to! Most of the information in this book applies generally to both directions. If the MTF point of view dominates, that's because that is the direction I went. In a few places where it became too cluttered syntactically to cover both cases, for example when discussing spouses, I've simply resorted to writing from the MTF perspective. I'll let you FTM guys figure out how it applies in your case. I know you'd want it that way, you are such a gallant bunch.

Please note that I do not have any professional training in this area. I am not a doctor, psychologist, or lawyer. (I do hold college degrees in computer engineering and business, but that is neither here nor there.) My expertise comes from having changed sex myself, from talkng with a lot of other people who have changed their sex, and from reading the same books that you can read yourself. Please consult with appropriate professionals rather than relying on any advice I give in this book. As a matter of fact, there is woefully little hard data on many of the issues facing transsexual people, so we are forced to make many of our decisions based on rumor, anecdotal evidence, tradition, and folklore. I probably should preface almost everything I say in this book with, "In my humble opinion…"; but that would get rather cumbersome.

Whether you are on the long, exciting road to a sex change, or a short hop to a cross-dressing hobby, or just curious, I hope you enjoy learning about *How To Change Your Sex*. I imagine that most of you will never change your sex; but perhaps you will be inspired to make other changes to your body or your life—maybe something that has long been a dream of yours. Three things that every transsexual person knows well are these: Change is possible; miracles do happen; and life is short, so you'd better start making your dreams come true today!

1 Are you transsexual?

So you think you are transsexual? Or maybe you don't know about that, but there's something appealing to you about passing as the other gender? The good news is that you don't need to figure out if you are transsexual right now. It's not important until you get to Chapter 7 or 8. Just relax and have fun for now. But you will want to be looking for the signs as you go along, so we'd better discuss the issue up front.

The odds are that you are not transsexual. The fact that you are reading this book indicates that you have at least a little bit of confusion or curiosity about your gender. That is not unusual; something like half of all people do. But only about one in 250 people is transsexual, and only a small number of them actually go about changing their sex. So rest assured that you are probably perfectly normal, and try to have some fun exploring your gender. If you are a guy, go ahead and try on your wife's sexy lingerie. (Ask her permission first!) If you're a gal, be a guy-type lumberjack or biker for a day. There's no harm in it, and you'll probably enjoy it.

On the other hand, suppose you won the lottery and you actually are transsexual. How do you know for sure? What does it even mean, to be transsexual?

The latter question, at least, is simple to answer. Being transsexual just means that you have the genitals appropriate for a particular sex, but your brain tells you that you are the other gender. In other words, you have a penis but you feel that you are a woman, or you have a vagina but you feel that you are a man. This is known in the psych books as Gender Identity Disorder, or GID. It causes anxiety, confusion, shame and guilt in the afflicted individual. These uncomfortable feelings, called gender dysphoria or GD, may be strong enough to prevent the transsexual person from forming successful social and intimate relationships or coping with life in a healthy manner.

Some people, who may be described as intersex or hermaphrodite, are born with ambiguous genitalia or various chromosomal anomalies which may also cause them to suffer feelings of gender dysphoria. A sex change may be appropriate treatment for some of these individuals. However, intersex is less common than transsexualism and the challenges and issues which confront these people are different than those faced by transsexuals; I do not attempt to address them in this book.

The best science to date indicates that transsexualism comes about because when your were just a little fetus developing in your mother's womb, your genitals started down the path towards one gender but a few weeks later the hormones took an unusual turn and your brain started down the path to the other gender. It is perfectly natural, if somewhat rare. It is nobody's fault and nothing to be ashamed of.

The tricky part is that you may not know what gender you really feel like. If you were born with a penis, like I was, chances are that you were raised as a boy, like I was. We got very strong messages from our parents and from society that we were boys, and you may think that is what you are, even if your brain is really female. How do you figure out where your true self lies? I'll show you how, seriously, in a moment. But first, here are some lighthearted clues to look for:

- ♥ If you are a guy and you like wearing women's clothing, you just might be transsexual. (If you are a gal and you like wearing men's clothing, don't worry, you're perfectly normal.)

- ♥ When you were a little boy, did you tell your mother, "I'm a girl!"? Maybe you are transsexual, and you were right after all! (About 80 per cent of transsexuals seem to have been aware of their gender issues from a very early age. Others, like me, may not realize it until they are 46 years old.)

- ♥ Does your sexual preference run strongly to loving women? You just might be transsexual! ...or lesbian; or both. Many male to female transsexuals start out liking women, and a large number of them never change, even if they do change their sex.

- ♥ Do your genitalia seem wrong to you? Maybe it's because they don't match the gender your brain feels, and you are transsexual.

- ♥ When you make love, do you fantasize that you are the other gender? Maybe it's because you are transsexual.

- ♥ If you've always felt more comfortable in groups of the other gender, maybe it's because your true gender is not what you thought it was.

- ♥ If you develop computer games for a living, you just may be transsexual. (The trans population boasts an unusually high number of software engineers. Might this indicate a relationship between transsexualism and creativity and intelligence? Some people think so.)

- ♥ Did your wife's first husband leave her and become a woman? Maybe that is your path too. Many ex-wives of transsexuals seem to wind up with another transsexual person or cross-dresser as their next mate, often to their own surprise.

♥ Is your brother a woman? You may be too! I know two sets of brothers who both had sex changes. Now they are sisters! (The link between genetics and transsexualism is being studied.)

Seriously, I don't believe that you can determine whether you are transsexual by taking a test or checking any list of symptoms. I, for example, never experienced any of the symptoms listed above, except for the wearing-women's-clothing thing—a symptom which is shared by many non-transsexual cross-dressers, and *not* experienced by a large number of true transsexuals. Oh, I also had the liking-women thing. (Now I prefer men.)

Becoming a firefighter

I believe that the only effective way to figure out if you are transsexual is a process of trying on different roles and seeing which ones feel like they fit you the best. It's the same for finding out anything about your true self. For example, suppose you think you would make a good firefighter. Start by studying up on firefighting. Read some books, watch some movies. Does it still appeal to you? Study it in more depth, so you really understand what it's all about. Does it still seem like what you would like to do with your life? Can you take the bad parts along with the good? Try it out. Do some firefighter-type activities in your spare time. (Be careful not to burn down your house when you do this!) Hang out at a fire station and buddy up with some real firefighters. If you are of age, find a bar where firefighters go for a drink after work and try to get to know them. Are they your kind of people? Can you see yourself doing what they do? If you still think firefighting is your calling, enroll in firefighter school, and get serious about it. Become a firefighter. After you've fought a few real fires, you will finally know for sure whether you were right, that firefighting is the life for you. You will be a firefighter.

You may not want to be a firefighter; but you do want to figure out if you are transsexual. How can you apply a similar process? Here are the steps. Keep in mind that your goals are to understand your true self, to have fun, and to enjoy your life. If at any time you feel uncomfortable, stop! You don't need to go any further.

1. Study up on transsexualism and transgenderism. You are reading this book; that's a good start. Try *The Lazy Crossdresser* by Charles Anders for another fun, helpful read. Watch these movies, if you can find them: Normal, an HBO movie; *Just Like A Woman;* and *Different For Girls. (Tootsie* and *Mrs. Doubtfire* are fun, but they won't help you very much I'm afraid. They are not very realistic. *To Wong Foo, Thanks for Everything! Julie Newmar* and *Priscilla, Queen of the Desert* are fun, too, but they're primarily about drag queens, not transsexuals.)

2. Now that you know a bit about it, does cross-dressing seem fun and exciting to you? Or, if not cross-dressing, maybe just leaving your gender markers behind and

becoming androgynous? Then why not try it out? Go to Chapter 2 in this book—*Getting started: Dressing and going out*. It will help get you going with cross-dressing or dressing androgynously; and give you some leads on how to get connected with support groups on the Internet and where to meet transgender folks (transsexuals, cross-dressers, and other gender border-crossers) in the real world.

3. Do you still think there's a chance that you are transsexual? Study it in more depth, so you really understand what it's all about. Read some more serious books, like *True Selves: Understanding Transsexualism - For Families, Friends, Coworkers, and Helping Professionals* by Mildred Brown and Chloe Rounsley. Try to meet some transsexual folks who are in the process of changing their sexes, or have already done so. Start seeing a therapist who specializes in gender issues—more on this in Chapter 6.

4. Are you starting to think that you really might be transsexual? (Or, if you knew it all along, do you still know it?) Can you take the bad parts along with the good? Good. Okay, now start part time cross-living. Spend more and more of your time in your new gender role doing regular activities like shopping and going to church, not just going on "adventures." Try to really think of yourself as a woman rather than a cross-dressed man when you are in your femme persona. Does it feel right to you? Does your old gender role feel wrong to

you? If so, it may be time to start taking some serious steps down the path to changing your sex.

5. If cross-living feels right to you and you are ready to abandon your old gender role completely, it's pretty likely that you are transsexual and ready to transition. (" Transition" is the word we use to describe the entire, gradual process of changing your sex.) Move on to Chapter 7: *Hormones,* and Chapter 8: *Transition.*

6. If you've allowed time for the hormones to change your chemical balances and you have become comfortable living and working full-time in your new gender, then you are ready for the final step: Become a firefighter. No, wait, that's not right. I mean, have sex reassignment surgery. Or don't. It's totally optional. Whatever feels right to you. Whether you do or whether you don't, it doesn't really matter. In either case, you are now living happily and successfully in your new, true gender. Congratulations, you have changed your sex! And now, at last, you know the answer: Yes, you were transsexual. However, you are not transsexual anymore. Now you're just a woman or a man, whichever the case may be, and you have no more gender confusion.

To recap, I recommend that you do not worry about whether or not you are truly transsexual as you start out. Keep it in the back of your mind as a possibility, but put your main energy into getting in touch with how you feel about the different identities you try on and the various activities you engage in. It may be months or even years before you need to seriously answer the "transsexual?" question—before you start taking any irrevocable actions. Even if the answer comes up, "No, I'm not transsexual," you will have discovered a great deal about your true self and opened your life up to a new honesty and some exciting new interests and directions.

Remember, there are no time limits on this. You are living your life, not trying to complete a project. You can always change your mind and decide, "Yes, I am transsexual" at any time in the future. But once you decide "Yes" and take certain extremely serious steps, like sex reassignment surgery or coming out at work, going back to "No" can be problematic, to say the least!

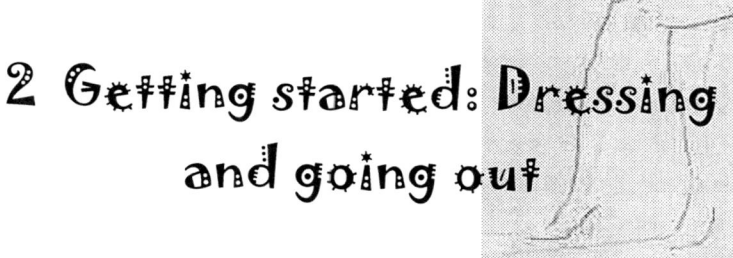

2 Getting started: Dressing and going out

Haven't you always wondered how the other half live? Why not find out? Go ahead! If you're a guy, try on a dress or some sexy lingerie. If you're a gal, chances are that you've already worn "male" clothes, but have you actually pretended to be a guy? Go ahead and do it. It's completely legal in all 50 of the United States in the 21st century, and it's perfectly moral in 72% of the world's major religions. Okay, I made up the figure about religions. You'll have to work out the morality issue in your own head. Take this, if it helps: I say it's not a moral issue, and I give you permission to do it!

It was easy for me to type the preceding paragraph today. But there was a time, not so very long ago, that it would have been the furthest thing from my mind. Nothing I learned growing up, even through the sexually-permissive '60s, so much as hinted at that sort of freedom of gender presentation. It was so far off the map that it was unspoken, although a thousand clues in daily life constantly enforced the idea that men are men and women are women, and that boundary must not be crossed. One day a little light went on in my head, and I said, "Why not cross the gender boundary?" And I never looked back.

Cross-dressing is fun—for a lot of people; not just transsexuals (and not for all transsexuals—more on that in a moment), but also for many others in the transgender community: cross-dressers, drag queens, female impersonators, and the simply curious. ("Transgender" is an umbrella term that includes all of these categories of gender-enhanced people.) If it holds absolutely no appeal for you whatsoever, then forget about it. But if it holds even a little appeal, why not give it try?

You probably want to do your initial cross-dressing experiments in private, unless you are lucky enough to have a very understanding spouse or friend; or, best of all, if you happen to have a friend who cross-dresses. You may actually dress in a closet, but if you do it in your bedroom with the curtains closed when nobody is at home, we still refer to this as being "in the closet."

Getting some clothes

When you start experimenting with cross-dressing, please do not "borrow" clothes that don't belong to you. Oh, many of us borrowed something from our mothers' or sisters' wardrobes or the laundry hamper when we were small, but adults should not do that. Spouses, in particular, get justifiably annoyed if they find their clothes or cosmetics mussed up, stretched out of shape, or soiled. The good news is that it is easy to get your own stuff. You can buy inexpensive clothes at mass market stores like Ross or Wal-Mart, or, better yet, thrift stores and Goodwill. I guarantee you that the people at the check-out counter will not give you any grief about buying clothes of the "wrong" gender. I used to prepare elaborate stories for inquisitive sales people; my most cunning one was about a wife who was too sick to do her own shopping, poor thing. I never had occasion to use my stories, thank goodness. At worst, sales clerks may make an assumption and say something like, "Your wife will like that!" Some cross-buyers take wicked pleasure in replying, "No, it's for me!"

If you are very intimidated about buying cross-gender clothes in person, then try shopping by mail-order catalog or the Internet. These outlets also are great sources for larger-sized items, if you are too big for the things that are usually on the racks in the women's stores. Of course, you need a discrete shipping address if you don't want your wife and kids to ask curious questions about your purchases. Be careful about having things shipped to your work address—your gregarious secretary is apt to ask your wife how she enjoyed her present from Victoria's Secret! (Maybe you shouldn't be hiding things from your wife in the first place? More on that coming up soon...)

The thrill of dressing / the androgyne way

Some transsexual people get a big thrill out of cross-dressing during the period prior to changing their sex. I cross-dressed thoroughly and enthusiastically for many years myself. Others cross-dress, but only because it feels comfortable and natural. That's the way I feel about dressing as a woman now; but, of course, it is not cross-dressing for me anymore. Cross-dressing would be if I tried to pass as a man. Yuck!

On the other hand, many transsexual people have no interest in the clothes aspect of it at all, or in strongly typing as either gender. They like to affect an androgynous look—neither identifiably male or female. These folks are often delighted when people seem confused about whether to call them "Sir" or "Ma'am." Over time they find that more and more people seem to call them by a new set of pronouns, and they say, "Hmmm, I guess I'm a woman [or a man] now." These two different approaches to migrating one's gender presentation usually end up at about the same place eventually, a more-or-less average, very passable appearance. Androgynous types of transsexuals very gradually change from presenting as one gender, to androgynous, to the other gender. We cross-dressing types change abruptly from one gender presentation to the other, and we often overshoot the mark. Initially our new gender presentation is likely to be overly femme (or overly butch), and gradually we learn to scale it back until we achieve a natural presentation in our new gender.

The androgyne path is often preferred by those who have the good fortune to transition at an early age, say the late teens or early twenties. Perhaps this is because young people's desires to fit in with their peers and not stand out as unusual are so strong. An androgynous presentation is something of a blank canvas upon which the beholder can paint whatever picture he or she chooses. If it works out well, family and friends can be swept along by your gradual feminization, and the shock will not be so great when one day you announce that you plan to change your sex.
Transitioning in middle age, like I did, has a distinctly different flavor. As adults our need for external approval is not so strong, so we can tolerate the inevitable odd looks and jibes we receive when we go out cross-dressed. Besides, the middle-aged, closeted, transsexual person often has no peer group or close friends to worry about anyway, because our life-long gender dysphoria has prevented us from forming healthy social relationships. Another factor is that we feel we have let too much of our lives slip by us already; we are anxious to get going in our fully femme presentation as quickly as possible, so the cross-dressing route appeals to us. It may also be that our identities, even if they are primarily masks behind which we hide our true selves, are so solidly formed that the abrupt, extreme shock of cross-

dressing is needed to crack them open and allow change to begin; whereas a younger person's more malleable self identity adapts more readily to the gradual molding process of an androgynous transition.

Androgyny is not always a stepping stone to transition. Some people who may identify as androgynes choose to eschew male/female gender typing completely and permanently, living their entire lives in an androgynous gender presentation. They may consider themselves to be both male and female genders at once; or neither; or something completely different. Sometimes their sexuality is celibate; or, even more than celibacy, a total disinterest in sex. In some cases their androgyny may be a response to having been born physically intersex—having ambiguous genitalia and/or rare chromosomal syndromes. Whatever the cause, androgyny is a valid and respectable life choice. It presents a different set of challenges and issues than transsexuality, and I don't try to cover it in this book. If you if you think you may be this type of person, you may want to look into support groups such as The Intersex Society of North America (www.isna.org).

Going out

If you enjoyed the experience of trying on a new gender presentation in the privacy of your own closet, your next step is to try out your new image on some other people. This will probably be the scariest thing you've ever done in your life! (Unless you are a battle-tried war veteran; I'm told that

Getting started: Dressing and going out 21

being shot at is much more scary.) I know it was terrifying for me; but it was also thrilling and rewarding.

There's no hurry about going out. As long as you are enjoying your activities in private, and you're not miserable in the rest of your life because of your gender confusion, then just stay in the closet. But there may come a point at which your feel "all dressed up and no place to go." Take heart; there are plenty of places to go.

There are a several good ways to take your new gender presentation out the front door (or, perhaps, the back door?). You can go to transgender support groups, transgender-friendly businesses, transgender-friendly nightclubs, or you can be a do-it-yourself-er. Traveling by car or plane can get you even further out, with even greater thrills and fun.

Transgender support groups

Most major cities have groups where transgender people meet for fun and support. Some, like Transgender San Francisco (TGSF), are mainly organized around social activities. TGSF has monthly dinners and the annual Cotillion where Miss TGSF and Mr. TGSF are crowned. Others, like Santa Cruz Trans and SCOUT (Santa Cruz Organization Uniting Trans men), both in Santa Cruz, California, are more oriented towards support and discussing personal issues. All of these organizations welcome new members, and you should feel free drop in wearing your regular clothes if you are not comfortable going out "dressed." Every group has its own personality and its own set of interesting characters, so don't be dismayed if you don't feel at home in the first group you visit. You might want to find another group in the next city over and give them a try. Transgender support groups are a great way to start meeting all different types of transgender people, and to try out your new gender presentation when you are brave enough.

Transgender-friendly businesses

You may be lucky enough to have a transgender-friendly business which does "transformations" or "makeovers" in your community. These are places where you can walk in as a man and walk out as a woman; or, just hang around the shop for while as a woman, if you prefer. (I don't know of any female to male makeover services. I guess FTMs are too smart to need 'em!) Carla's in San Jose, California is one of the most famous of these establishments. The Hidden Woman in Reno, Nevada is another. The Hidden Woman even has package deals for Las Vegas—a nice little vacation idea.

These "transformation" services tend to be a bit pricey. If you can afford it, they're a nice way to get started. They are also great places to pick up tips on doing your makeup, wigs, and fashions. Even if you have been able to put yourself together reasonably well on your own, these shops are still fun destinations for you. You can visit them just to try out your new look while shopping and socializing. They are very open-minded and accepting no matter how

Getting started: Dressing and going out

undeveloped your look may be, and they are great places to meet other transgender people.

One day I discovered how very understanding and accommodating of special needs such shops can be. I was in Carla's one afternoon doing a little shoe-shopping and I met a gorgeous Chinese girl—who was actually a guy, of course. She was tall, thin, absolutely lovely, and fun to chat with. I was surprised to find out that she had never dressed as a woman until Carla had transformed her that afternoon. I was even more astonished to realize, after I had been chatting and waling around the shop with her for about a half hour, that she was completely blind!

Transgender-friendly nightclubs

Another way to take your new gender presentation out into the world is to be a vampire! Vampires are cross-dressers who come out only after dark. There are many t-girls (transgender girls) whose feminine selves never see the light of day. Clubbing is their life.

Very few bars and nightclubs cater exclusively to transgenders. Even in San Francisco, that mecca of sexual deviance, only two of the over 100 clubs in the city have transgender themes: Diva's, a bar and dance club, and AsiaSF, a bar and restaurant featuring beautiful transsexual waitresses. So mostly transgender club kiddies make do with gay bars.

You are not likely to find transgender folks in every gay bar. In fact, gays and lesbians are usually no more familiar with transgenders (other than drag queens) than the general population. Nevertheless gay bars are—usually—friendly and accepting of transgenders. If you feel uneasy about going into a gay bar, I've got news for you. Whenever I go into gay bars I see women there, and heterosexual couples too. In lesbian bars, I see some men and some couples. Heck, the gay bars have the best dance music, and all the serious club kiddies know it! So don't be afraid to drop into a few of your local gay drinking establishments and ask the bartenders whether t-girls hang out there. Ask which night—sometimes we gather at particular pubs on specific nights of the week or month. For example, San Francisco's most wonderful transgender party is Trannie Shack, which is held every Tuesday night at The Stud bar south of Market. ("Trannie" is slang for "transgender person." Sometimes it is spelled "tranny", but I prefer "trannie" because, well, my nickname is "Lannie the Trannie"!) If a bar doesn't have a trans clientele, just ask the bartender if he knows where else we go in town. He'll know.

When you are out clubbing after dark, please be careful! Danger lurks everywhere these days, and you are especially vulnerable in your new gender presentation. Be aware of what is going on around you, and don't trust strangers. Don't provoke or challenge people; if you are provoked or teased, just walk away. Don't assume that the police will help you; if you are obviously a cross-dresser or transsexual person, the police, sadly, may look the other way when you are in trouble. Be especially careful if you are drinking or otherwise "partying," and don't drink too much. Don't drink and drive! If the police stop you when you are obviously cross-dressed or transsexual, it could go either of two ways. One school of thought is that you are likely to be sent on your way because no cop wants the rest of the guys at the station house to see him filling out paper work on a trannie all night; another school of thought is that they are more likely to run you in just for the fun of it. Why take a chance?

Be a do-it-yourself-er

You don't need support groups, or trans-friendly businesses, or trannie bars to go out. You can just be a normal person and go the mall. As a bonus, you can shop for more clothes and shoes while you're there. I did just that for many years. You will be surprised at how little attention you receive. Be sure to dress "merge", that is, so that you merge in with rest of the crowd. Don't go to the mall dressed like a five dollar hooker if you don't want to attract attention. (Five dollar hookers dress that way specifically to attract attention.)

Look for trans-friendly public events in your area. Most communities host an LGBT (lesbian gay bisexual transsexual) Pride celebration in June each summer. This is an ideal environment in which to try out your new gender presentation. If you get clocked, just be proud! Similarly friendly events include San Francisco's Folsom Street Fair, which is held on the last Sunday in September and features a heavy dosage of leather and bondage arts and crafts; and the Transgender San Francisco (TGSF) Cotillion, where Miss and Mr. Transgender San Francisco are selected each

January. (Granted, San Francisco may have more LGBT-themed events than most communities.)

If you begin your going-out activities in transgender-friendly environments or as a vampire, be sure to get some real-world experience too, if you think you really might be transsexual. If you change your sex, you won't be able to spend your life in bars and support groups. Going to the movies is a great initial adventure in the real world—a few moments of panic while you buy your ticket, two hours enjoying yourself out but alone in the dark, and then a few more moments of panic as you exit the theater and walk to your car. Parks and museums are great places to be a do-it-yourself-er. Some churches like Unity, Unitarian, and Metropolitan Community Church (MCC) emphasize diversity and welcome transgender worshipers at their services and events. Flea markets, summer arts and crafts festivals, and free outdoor concerts are fun places to mingle with the regular folk.

Travel and conventions

Traveling en femme can be enjoyable and exciting adventures. Driving around town without even leaving your car provides a safe environment for your initial steps out of the closet. I still remember the thrill of my first drive over the hill to visit a friend at Santa Cruz beach, with absolutely no boy clothes in my possession, not even for emergencies! As you grow more confident in your new gender presentation, you may want to try longer road trips and even plane trips. If you go somewhere where you are unlikely to run into anyone you know, you may find more courage to flaunt your new image. So what if you get clocked (recognized as a cross-dresser)? You'll never see those people again.

Transgender conventions are especially good destinations for out of town trips. Transgender people from all over the world gather annually in late September at a fine hotel in Atlanta, Georgia for Southern Comfort Conference (SCC), the largest and most famous such convention. Meetings and activities are scheduled throughout the week, though many people attend Thursday through Sunday or just for the weekend. SCC is a great opportunity to spend several days or a whole week entirely in your new gender identity. During the day you can attend sessions on diverse topics of interest to the transgender community, such as transgender activism, feminine style and deportment, sex reassignment surgery, dealing with families, and many other subjects. Lunch and dinner provide great opportunities to make new friends as everybody socializes together in a large banquet room. In the evenings and occasionally during the day buses arrive to take groups to pre-arranged entertainments such as shopping, nightclubs, and shows. A Big Brother/Sister program teams experienced people with newbies to help with those first scary, tentative steps out the hotel room door.

Other popular transgender conventions in the U.S. include Esprit, held near Seattle in May; Colorado Gold Rush in Denver in March; and the less formal but more fun Diva Las Vegas in May in Sin City itself.

A lot of people worry about traveling in a gender presentation which does not match the gender on their identification documents, especially with the stepped-up airport security since the 9/11 tragedy. I don't think this is really a problem. The first time I flew presenting as female but with male id was when I traveled to Southern Comfort just a couple of weeks after 9/11/2001. My best friend, Jamie Faye Fenton, remembers that I seemed extremely nervous as we headed for the airport! A guard at a security checkpoint studied my driver's license carefully, then looked me up and down. Finally, he smiled and said, "You've lost a lot of weight, haven't you?" "Yes!" I agreed, and scurried through the metal detector.

A lot of people travel with mismatched gender on their id all the time and they rarely encounter difficulties. Just be sure to be totally honest if anyone questions you or asks for your id. I've found that saying, "I'm transsexual" is a magic password—security people have been trained to understand this and let you through. *Never try to use a fake id!* As insurance, you may want to carry a letter from your therapist explaining your condition; we jokingly call this a "Get Out Of Jail Free" card and it may help in some sticky situations. If you want to be really careful, you may want to be prepared to quick-change back to "guy mode" if airport authorities insist on it.

That said, I should mention the story of Sarah West, a delightful English girl who traveled to the United States for Southern Comfort Conference in 2000. On her way home she boarded a United Airlines connecting flight in Omaha, Nebraska. UA personnel pulled her off the plane, which she had already boarded, and forced her to change into male clothes to match her British passport. She even had a "Get Out Of Jail Free" card, a letter from eminent British psychiatrist Dr. Russell Reid, but it was no help in this situation. Sarah was humiliated and sued the airline, but her timing was unfortunate; the lawsuit got derailed in United's bankruptcy mess following the 9/11 disaster a year later. Sarah has traveled extensively in the United States and Europe without any other trouble, but you should be aware that incidents like this may occur from time to time.

Getting connected

If you follow the do-it-yourself approach to going out exclusively, you are unlikely to meet other transgender people. That's too bad, because you do want to meet other transgender folks so you can compare stories, get ideas about your gender identity and presentation, and know that there are others who share your feelings. Fortunately, there are other ways to get connected in the transgender community.

Sometimes it seems that there are more transgender and transsexual people around today than ever before. I don't think the incidence of gender confusion is any greater today than it used to be. What is different is the Internet. Thanks to the World Wide Web, we have been able to connect with each other and find out that we are not alone. We have been able to share information about our condition and to encourage each other to explore our diversity and enjoy our gender-enhanced lives. You can too. Just google "transgender support groups," "transgender-friendly businesses, " and "transgender friendly nightclubs" for plenty of links to the types of places I discussed in this chapter. (You do know that to "google" means to use the Internet search engine at www.google.com, don't you?) Google "transgender" and "transsexual" for plenty of other useful information. Look for transgender-related groups under the "group" features of the Yahoo, Google, and MSN portals. Check out some online e-zines like Transgender Forum (www.tgforum.com), which publishes articles by your humble author (that's me!) every month. Sample a lot of different transgender communities, groups, and resources to get a feel for the wonderful diversity within our community; sometimes it may seem that all trannies are impoverished, or rich, or hookers, or pathetic, or stunning; but keep looking, and eventually you will find somewhere where you feel like you belong.

The Internet is great for finding a lot of other things you will want as well. Makeup and fashion tips are easily located. Advice on special trannie needs, like breast forms and prosthetic penises, beard cover, and tucking (concealing the penis by tucking it between the legs) are available. Online shopping provides an easy way to assemble your new wardrobe, assuming you have a place to discretely receive packages. Try www.payless.com (Payless ShoeSource—I love it because sizes up to 13 are available mail-order from their Web site) for shoes and www.onehanesplace.com for nylons and brassieres, for example; try www.carabella.com for sexy dresses. For more exotic attire, Frederick's of Hollywood and Victoria's Secret probably jump into your mind; but you can visit plenty of other fine boutiques like www.threewisheslingerie.com and www.ladybwear.com as well.

If and when you get serious about actually changing your sex, you'll want to visit these two well-respected sites: Andrea James's *TS Roadmap* www.tsroadmap.com and Dr. Anne Lawrence's *Transsexual Women's Resources* www.annelawrence.com/twr. You might also want to look in at *FemImage* www.femimage.com/ where the lovely and amazing Denaë Doyle provides a unique service coaching trans women on feminine poise and deportment.

Feel free to post to the group discussion boards and to e-mail people you meet online. You will find some nice people, a few mean ones, and a lot who will just ignore you. So what? You are anonymous online, and it's worth the effort to find the nice ones. If you arrange to meet anyone in 3-D (that is, in person in the three dimensional world), take the usual precautions you would in meeting any stranger, no matter how well you may feel you have gotten to know them online. It's best to meet in a public place; trans social events and support groups are great meeting places. As a rule of thumb, psycho killers like to remain anonymous so they are unwilling to meet you in a group situation. (But don't stake your life on that assumption.)

A very pleasant aspect of being transgender is that it is very easy to make friends within the transgender community. You instantly share a deep and intimate bond with your trans sisters and brothers, so there is always something to talk about to break the ice. It is easy to get close very quickly. However, don't be surprised if your new friends also fade from your life very quickly. This happens because, once you get past the superficial similarities of the both of you being cross-dressers or transsexual, you find that you don't have much else in common. Also, a lot of people in the trans community are changing very rapidly—and you most quickly of all, as you go through with actually changing your sex. So it is not unusual to find that you have grown out of relationships that you thought would last forever. This can be very difficult on you, especially as you will be on an emotional roller-coaster from the hormones and other changes in your life. But you have to accept it and more on, without taking it as a personal failure or insult. It is likely that some of the people you meet will remain your friends and allies for life, but it may only be at the level of the occasional e-mail or Christmas card.

You will meet some people in the transgender community who seem to be walking disaster areas. They have money problems, they can't find a job, their marriage is breaking up, they have health problems, and they have a million things they "need" to do for their transition. (Some of the ones with the most things to do for their transition wind up never actually changing their sex at all.) And they'll talk about nothing else. Then you'll meet others who seem to have it all—a good grasp on their identities, lives that are working well, and they look great. But don't be fooled. If you get a chance to know them well, you'll find out that all of us have our demons. The point is that you should not waste your energy being envious of anyone you meet, or excessively sorry for those who seem to be having rougher times. Just try to be a good, supportive friend, and we can all

Getting started: Dressing and going out

help each other through this. You might want to be particularly cautious about inviting down-and-out t-girls to share your residence. It is often much easier to get them to move in than it is to get them to move out again. On the other hand, sometimes t-girls make fine roommates, sharing expenses as well as joys and sorrows. Just be careful!

One final hint. Don't expect anybody to become all giddy at the prospect of helping *you* learn how to dress up. That's what transformation services are for.

Getting clocked

When you go out in public sporting your new gender presentation, you will be amazed to find that almost everyone will completely ignore you. I've run around in some of the most outrageous outfits, trying my best to get some attention, to no avail. Nevertheless, from time to time, you are going to be "clocked." Getting "clocked" or "read" means that somebody recognizes that you are not quite what you seem to be. Most of the time this comes in the form of overhearing somebody exclaim to their companion, "That's a man!" Less often someone will confront you with a question like, "Are you a man?"; or they'll try to be cute with a comment like, "Dude, nice dress!" Very rarely, at least in my experience, will somebody be actually hostile.

A transsexual person's desire to pass—not to be clocked—is completely understandable. A cross-dresser or a drag queen may not mind being clocked because they inwardly identify as men; it does not bother them to be recognized as such. In fact, most drag queens, those who dress in an outrageously exaggerated manner, expect and demand to be clocked. (But you had better treat them as ladies, or they will let you have it!) I, on the other hand, as a transsexual person, inwardly identify as a woman; it challenges my identity and hurts my feelings if somebody treats me like a man. If you have a strong feeling about passing, it may be an indication that you tend toward the transsexual side of things.

Who is most likely to clock you? Teenage girls are absolutely the best at clocking t-girls. They are self-conscious and are constantly evaluating other women as they strive to develop their own feminine images and personalities. (As trans women we go through much the same process, though we need to move rapidly from our psychological teenage years to something more befitting our real ages.) Fortunately, teenagers are so wrapped up in their own little worlds that they rarely notice us if we are older. Men are terrible at clocking t-girls because their attention is always focused on our bosoms and legs, which are usually our best features. The funniest clocking incidents are when a small child looks up at her mother and says, "Mommy, why is that man wearing a dress?" Little kids' eyes see directly into our souls.

One big factor that causes t-girls to get clocked is their tendency to dress inappropriately or to overdress. Ridiculously short skirts, sexy heels, large breast forms, and long, flowing wigs are alluring, but they will attract attention in the mall—especially if you are 55 years old, six feet four inches tall, and 280 pounds. The urge to dress this

Getting started: Dressing and going out

way is often part of the Cinderella complex, or "feminine overshoot": having finally granted yourself permission to wear feminine clothes, permission you have denied yourself for so long, you want to go all out and wear the most sexy, outrageous outfits you can find. There is nothing wrong with this; just expect to get clocked a lot if you wear these outfits out in the conventional world. Maybe you'd be better off enjoying them in the privacy of your own home, or at trannie-friendly nightclubs? (You can wear absolutely anything at Trannie Shack!)

Incidentally, Halloween is a great opportunity to shop for femme clothes with confidence, and to have some of your first "going out dressed" adventures. But Halloween is also the worst day of the year for getting clocked, because people are looking for disguises and costumes on that day.

If you are worried about being clocked, you should be aware of the "Two Trannie Rule." The Two Trannie Rule says that the chances of being clocked go up exponentially with the number of t-girls in a group. Two t-girls together are four times as likely to be clocked as a single t-girl by herself; three t-girls are nine times as likely, etc. So expect to be clocked if you go out with a group of other transsexual women or cross-dressers. The situation in which you are least likely to be clocked is if you are out with a man, preferably one whom you do not tower over, because his presence validates you as a woman. If you are with a non-trans woman or a group of women, it can work in your favor because they accept you as one of their own, or it can work against you if the contrast between their femininity and yours is too great. If you go out with your spouse, there is an extra danger that you may fall into your accustomed male patterns and make it obvious that you are the husband.

My advice about getting clocked is simply this: Get used to it. It doesn't matter how good your gender presentation skills become, or how hot you are—even a hottie like me gets clocked now and then. It's not important to me. I'm not trying to fool anybody about anything. If they know what I really am, so what? The whole point of the exercise is to understand my true self, and to live as exactly that. Oh, don't get me wrong. It still hurts my feelings if someone thinks of me as a *man;* but it doesn't bother me if they know I'm a trans woman as long as they accept me as a woman.

I learned a good lesson about getting clocked when I was still just a cross-dresser (or so I thought). I was out at a "straight" dance club in San Francisco with two trans woman friends. We were leaving the club in the wee hours when a young fellow passed us on his way in. He gave us a classic double-take, his head swiveling around to give us a careful second look. Sounding incredulous, he asked, "Are you men?" My friends just laughed and replied in unison, "No, we're trannies!" and we blew on by. This taught me that I didn't need to hide in shame from my transgender nature; rather, I could and should be proud of it—or rather, proud of myself, in spite of it. It wasn't our problem—the guy was a goof for not realizing what was going on!

Ironically, once you don't care about getting clocked anymore, that's when it stops happening. The number one key to passing is self-confidence. The number two key is a big smile. These are the only tools that will ever get you a pass from a small child. Until you develop the confidence to present comfortably in your new gender identity, here is a prescription for faking it: walk slowly; breathe deeply; and look people in the eyes.

When nature calls

When you venture out in public in your new gender presentation, there will come a time when you feel a call of nature. Which restroom should you use? The general guideline is to use the restroom appropriate for the gender in which you are presenting yourself. So if you are a guy going out dressed as a woman, use the ladies' room. If you're a gal passing as a guy, use the men's room. Your primary concern should be your personal safety. A cross-dressed person (guy or gal) could get beat up if they get clocked in a men's room. If you sense that risk, don't go in. It is less likely that you will be assaulted in a women's room, but don't kid yourself, women can get rough, too; especially, say, in a dyke leather bar.

If you're not completely comfortable using the restroom, or if your gender presentation isn't highly passable, then do your business and get out as quickly as possible. Don't dawdle at the mirror checking your makeup, or start conversations, etc. The restroom is is not the best place to make new friends.

If you go into a women's room and find that all the stalls are full and there is a line, don't panic. Just get in line and wait your turn. In general, if there is a problem using a restroom, the objections don't come from the women. The problem is that men don't want to think of a cross-dresser in the restroom with their wives—although what they imagine goes on in there, I can't fathom.

I'm not a legal expert, but I believe that in most states and municipalities, using a public restroom appropriate for your gender presentation but not your biological sex is perfectly legal. Nevertheless, you wouldn't want to have to prove it in court. Be discreet.

3 Sex, Part 1

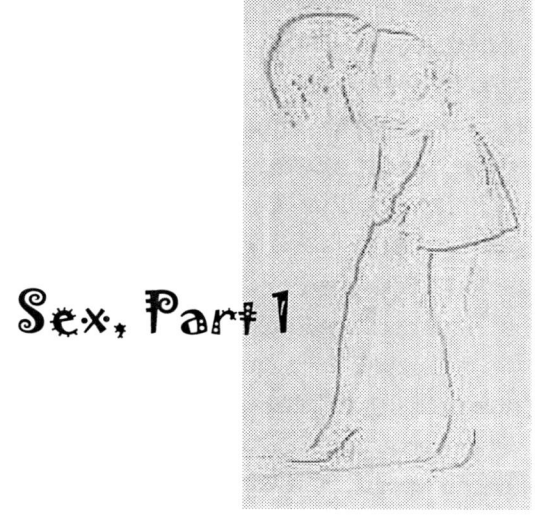

More good news! You don't have to change your sexual orientation just because you change your sex. If you're a man who loves women today, you can be a woman who loves women tomorrow. If you're a woman who loves women today, you can be a man who loves women tomorrow. It doesn't matter. Your sexual orientation is independent of your sex and your gender. Jamison Green, PlanetOut's "Visible Man" columnist, estimates that 40% of trans women identify as lesbian and 30% of trans men identify as gay men.

On the other hand, you just might find your sexual preference changing as you stretch the boundaries of your gender identity and gender expression. Don't worry, nobody is going to force you to change against your will. But the point of this journey is to discover and actualize your true self, right? It may be that the sexual preference with which you have been living is not your true self, it's just what society pressured you to be. We get very strong messages to be "normal" heterosexuals, so maybe you just followed direction well. Or maybe your are so heterosexual that you like girls when you are in a boy frame of mind, and you like boys when you are in a girl frame of mind; this could be described as "situational heterosexuality." Maybe you are open to sexual arousal regardless of what genitalic equipment happens to be involved; in which case you are bisexual, like me.

The possibilities of what may turn you on sexually are endless. Besides sexual preference, you may find that you have an interest in wearing leather, or getting tied up, or pretending you are a horse, or even having clown sex. (I am not making these things up!) How do you know where your true sexual interests lie? My advice is to experiment. Try as many things as possible; see what works for you and what doesn't. Alcohol and drugs (not that I would ever advocate *illegal* narcotics, mind you!) can be very useful in helping loosen your inhibitions during your experimentation phase.

I caution you to please be safe when you are experimenting sexually. This includes safe sex, to avoid nasty diseases and unwanted pregnancies; personal safety in terms of dealing only with people and in environments you know and can trust; and psychological safety, in not pushing yourself too far past the limits of your comfort zone. (Though stretching your comfort zone a little bit can be a good thing.)

What does sexual experimentation have to do with changing your sex? It's not a direct connection. In fact, some people choose to maintain a celibate lifestyle while they deal with their gender issues, and even afterward. This is a perfectly legitimate choice. But humans are sexual beings, and it is not unusual—or shameful, or immoral—to have a desire to get in touch with your true sexuality as part of your exploration of your true self. I found it to be a very enriching aspect of changing my sex. Perhaps you will, too.

Specifically what might you do to explore your sexual nature? Here are some hints and ideas that I came across during my gender journey, and which seem common in the transgender community.

Sex play with other transgender people

Prior to realizing that I was transsexual, I thought I was a "normal" heterosexual man with a cross-dressing fetish. Eventually I began to make friends with other cross-dressers, and at some point friendship turned into sex play. At first I was quite turned off by penises—my own as well as those attached to others. I soon overcame that disinclination, however, and I found that I could enjoy sex play with another pretty t-girl in spite of all the penises involved. I guess that makes me bisexual. However, I never had a sexual encounter with a man while I was presenting as a man; that never appealed to me. So I guess I was "bisexual, with reservations."

Sex play with a t-girl is fun. It's like sex play with a sexy girl, except for that extra penis and a tendency to be more uninhibited than it usually is with your average non-t-girl. You should try it.

Notice that I use the phrase "sex play". Like Bill Clinton, I usually think of "sex" as meaning something involving penetration. There are plenty of pleasurable sexual activities you can enjoy which don't involve penetration. Kissing and petting, fondling and caressing, peek-a-boo, and dressing and undressing can all be great fun. Then there is oral sex.

Oral sex

People with penises (men and t-girls) love getting blow jobs. I never really understood the attraction myself; but you might expect that, seeing as I eventually had my own penis removed. I have a few ideas about why oral sex is so popular. One is that guys love getting blow jobs because they can't get them from their wives at home. Another is that it is because it does not require them to get and maintain firm erections; this can be a particular problem when there is a lot of alcohol involved, or if the person with the penis in question has been on hormones for a while. Yet another idea is that blow jobs are popular because the recipient gets to be completely selfish—no concern about the partner's needs for now!

One point I do understand is that *giving* oral sex can be a very affirming thing for a t-girl's new gender identity. Early in my own sexual explorations, giving a guy a blow job made me feel very feminine and desirable. Now, it only validates my feeling that men like blow jobs. In any case, oral sex is good, relatively clean fun, so enjoy it if you are so inclined.

Of course, there is also oral sex of the vaginal/clitoral variety, i.e., cunnilingus. That's fun too; especially on the receiving end, if I may say so.

Oh yes; it's been said before, but it is worth repeating: you don't actually blow on it!

Anal sex

Good news! You don't have to have anal sex. (You don't have to do anything you don't want to, but it seems especially worth mentioning in this particular regard.) Some transgender girls enjoy anal sex, but many do not. Why not? Because it hurts. Ouch! I guess it doesn't hurt so much after a while, when your sphincter muscle learns to relax, but initially it is quite painful. (I'm thinking of selling a bumper sticker that reads, "Caution! Objects in the anus may feel larger than they appear." You could put it on your headboard as a reminder.) If it sounds like something you'd like to try, now that I've made it sound so inviting, go right ahead. Remember to use a condom, and that there is no such thing as too much lube. If you want to keep away from this activity, that's perfectly fine; we won't revoke your transgender card.

Sex play with admirers

Men who have a thing for t-girls are referred to as "t-girl admirers" or "trannie chasers." Usually they are mainly interested in having sex. In particular, like most people with penises, they love blow jobs; surprisingly, they are often more enthused about giving them to you than getting them from you. Some admirers—not many, but some—are sincerely interested in socializing, not just sex. A few wonderful, sweet guys actually want t-girls for regular girlfriends. Admirers can be fun to play with. Just be sure in your own mind of what you expect out of the relationship; don't be hurt by a guy who's just out for sex if you're looking for a real boyfriend. Remember that you always have the right to say "No!" and to set boundaries of how far you are willing to go.

By the way, you're not gay if at least one of the participants is in a dress, regardless of the number of penises involved. This principle is very important to most trannie chasers.

Vaginal sex

Penetrative vaginal sex is universally found to be fun. If you are t-girl, you may find that GGs (genetic girls, the kind born with vaginas) are attracted to you; we would call these women female trannie chasers. Some t-girls seem to be GG magnets. Others, like me, never seem to run into receptive GGs. If you do have the opportunity to have sex with a GG while in your feminine mode, you may find that it takes on a different character than the sex you have as a man. It may feel more like lesbian sex to you. Many t-girls think of themselves as male lesbians. On the other hand, it may feel just like regular sex except that you are in a dress; you may find yourself reverting completely to your male behaviors and feelings once sex play begins.

If you are a t-boy (a transgender boy) with a vagina of your own, there are many possibilities for vaginal sex; I am sure you don't need me to enlighten you on that subject.

Toys

If you've never played with sex toys, that may be an area for you to explore in your new gender presentation. Sex toys mostly means dildos and vibrators of every shape and size, designed for use in vaginas and anuses, and including strap-on varieties. Surely you know what a strap-on is? It's a belt-like harness that you wear around your waist; it holds a dildo so you can use the dildo like a penis, without using your hands. A strap-on has obvious utility for a person with no penis of his or her own, but it can also be used by somebody with a penis. I find the concept of a strap-on on a person who already has a penis somewhat amusing, but it can compensate for the erectile problems that I mentioned before.

Some other types of sex toys that might interest you include beads and Ben Wa balls (or Duotone balls, my personal favorite) for use in the anus or vagina; butt plugs; clit simulators; various items for tickling, pinching, and clamping; penis rings and pumps; love dolls; and fake vaginas. If you are serious about sex dolls, be sure to check out www.realdoll.com where they sell very expensive, creepily realistic, silicone rubber love dolls. Fake vaginas are not just for the pleasure of lonely guys; artificial vaginas intended for cross-dressers and trans women are designed to conceal the penis and create the impression of a reasonably functional vagina.

Beyond these items, sex toys tend to fall into the next area I will mention, BDSM.

BDSM

BDSM, a cleverly overloaded acronym, stands for Bondage and Discipline, Dominance and Submission, Sadism and Masochism. People generally just say "Bondage" or " BDSM." Pretty scary sounding stuff, isn't it? I've observed some BDSM activity and even participated to a little extent. In actuality it's not very scary, but it certain practices can be rather revolting and there may be real pain involved.

BDSM activities typically take place in a room designated the "Dungeon." The dungeon is rarely deep in the earth beneath a castle. More likely it is a warehouse in an industrial section of town or a room in the back or upstairs at a club, or in a closet or a basement of a private house. Temporary dungeons may be set up for the night at dance clubs or parties. Often BDSM parties are private, invitation only affairs, and cameras are strictly forbidden for privacy reasons. The dungeon is filled with a variety of equipment for restraining participants, such as St. Andrew's Crosses, racks, and stocks. The dungeon may be well lighted or dim. It may be quiet, or Goth music may provide a creepy aural ambiance.

In the dungeon willing victims get tied up and spanked, flogged, and whipped. A person may prefer the "dom" or dominant role, doing the flogging, or the "sub" or submissive role, being the floggee. Some people switch between both roles as they feel like it. Other activities may include fire play with candles and lighter fluid, and edge play involving knives. Water and scat play, referring to excretory matter, is another category of entertainment, but it is rare because it requires special sanitation arrangements and a special taste for that sort of thing. (I personally have never witnessed edge, water, or scat play, and I plan to keep it that way.) Tying someone up—the bondage part of BDSM—can be an activity complete unto itself, exhibiting beautiful knot and rope work. Saran wrap is another popular binding material. (I once saw a beautiful t-girl, Charles Anders, author of *The Lazy Crossdresser*, wrapped neck-to-toe in yellow police DO NOT PASS tape; but this was a fashion statement, not bondage.)

BDSM activities are organized as "Scenes". In a typical scene, one dom will torture one sub on a particular piece of equipment. A scene may last from 15 minutes to an hour. The protocol is that nobody should interfere when a scene is going on. You are welcome to watch (that's part of the thrill for the scene's participants), but do not talk to the participants. The scene may involve additional people. It may be improvised or the participants may have a sequence of actions planned out. Typically a dom and a sub have a more or less standard routine that they like to go through all the time. The sub may be naked or stripped down to very few clothes.

It is important to understand that BDSM groups emphasize safety above all else. The dom and the sub negotiate activities and boundaries before starting a scene. A sub will only work with a dom she or he thoroughly trusts. The sub always has a safe word to signal to the dom that she or he should go easier or stop. (By default, the traffic light system is used: "Green" means okay, "Yellow" means slow down, "Red" means stop.) Potentially dangerous activities like fire or edge play are only performed by trained, professional doms. Often BDSM parties are drug and alcohol free. Of course, nothing is ever done without consent. If you find yourself in a dungeon, there is no chance that you will be grabbed and tied up against your will. In fact, you'll probably have a hard time finding someone willing to tie you up, if you didn't bring your own dom. So bring a friend (and your own ropes) if you want to do more than observe.

I was surprised to find that BDSM activities rarely include actual sex play. Occasionally genitalia and breasts are tortured, but I've never seen them fondled in a dungeon. Most dungeons have explicit rules against sex and total nudity. I am told that some BDSM'ers do include sex in their rituals, but that is in the privacy of their own homes, or in private clubs to which I have not been invited.

Beyond the simple joys of inflicting or receiving pain—if you go for that sort of thing—BDSM is grand playground of toys, costume, and equipment. Whips, paddles, floggers, cat-o-nine-tails, riding crops, rattan canes, and ball-gags abound. Leather harnesses, rubber, latex, and imaginative clothes of all types are plentiful. St. Andrew's Crosses (giant Xs) are the most popular binding equipment, but a creative collection of racks, tables, slabs, nets, and slings can be found, some featuring exquisite workmanship. There is some overlap between BDSM folks and the leather crowd, and with Goths, due to their common interest in the dark side. A fetish ball is a place where you can meet them all. This a special night at a dance club where everyone is encouraged to come in their wildest, fetishistic outfits; there may be a dungeon set up in back room or corner for BSDM play or demonstrations. San Francisco's *Exotic Erotic Ball* at Halloween is one of the largest and most famous fetish balls—but hardly the best!

BDSM is not, of course, a primarily transgender activity. In fact, the BDSM scene is populated mostly by "straight" people. But, in my experience, BDSM groups tend to be quite accepting of transgender people, and they are usually a bit excited by our presence. On the other hand, a lot of transgender people seem quite attracted to BDSM. So if you get the opportunity to visit a private BSDM dungeon or a public one at a fetish ball, go ahead and give it a try.

I have been stripped down to just my panties and flogged thoroughly on a few of occasions. I did not enjoy the pain, but I did discover that I've got a bit of an exhibitionist streak. I enjoyed entertaining the onlookers with my shrieks and my writhing, naked body!

Age play

Age play is for people who are turned on by dressing up and acting like little kids or even babies. Maybe you would look cute in a Catholic schoolgirl uniform? Get out your plaid skirt and starched white shirt. If you notice a pretty little underage schoolgirl at your next fetish ball, take a closer look; she could be 35 years old—and she could be a man!

Furries

"Furries" are people who like to be animals for the evening. Costumes range from simple to elaborate, and from cartoon-like to realistic. Horses (pony boys and pony girls) are a particular specialty. Cats are very common. I once saw a zebra at a fetish ball. Furries like to get in a big fur pile and scritch each other. It sounds like fun to me, although I've never had the opportunity to try it out. They hold conventions. You could go to one if you want to explore it.

Clown sex

Clowns scare me; but some people like to have sex while dressed up like clowns. Preferably twenty or thirty of them in the back seat of a tiny car—ha! I can't claim to understand this fetish, but the balloon animals are fun.

There is vast world of sexual variation and fun out there. Something is "bound" to turn you on, pun intended. Why not experiment a bit, and find out what lurks in your deepest libido? I didn't know anything about any of these things before I started on my own gender journey. Now I'm practically an expert; and no worse for the wear, I might add. Google can get you started with links about any of these activities, and much, much more. (Sex on the Internet? Who would have imagined such a thing?)

4 Your spouse and children

If you think being transgender is tough on you, stop for a moment and consider how hard it is on your spouse and children. (If you don't have a spouse or children, you can just skip this chapter.) It is probably the hardest thing that they will ever go through. It may be even harder on them than it is on you; at least you are in control of the situation to some extent. They are simply stuck with trying to cope. Every step you take in realizing your hidden feminine or masculine potential creates a big crack in the foundation of your spouse's happiness. As you go through your sex change, remember that your spouse or significant other and your children need your love—your time, your attention, and your support—now more then ever before. Also please keep in mind that your decision to present yourself in a new gender does not automatically release you from your marriage vows!

Quite a number of trans people have spouses and children at the time they discover they are transsexual. These are terribly tough situations for everybody. How unfair! Why would somebody who is transsexual marry somebody else under the pretense that he is "normal?" (Let's talk about the case of an MTF transsexual married to a genetic woman, lest the pronouns get out of hand; and I will refer to the MTF as "he" since he has not yet transitioned and is still presenting as a man.) How dare he bring children into it as well? The answer to these questions, in all the cases that I have heard of, is that the trans people had no idea of the paths their lives would take. They were trying their very best to live up to the expectations of their parents, of society, and of their own selves, to be the best "normal" men they could be. Even if they had an inkling—or a damn good understanding—that they were "different," they thought if they just lived "normal" lives, their transgender urges would go away and they could be "normal." Besides marrying and fathering children, these men often pursue very macho careers in the military, sports, the construction industry, and the like. I can assure you that this does not work. If you are a young person reading this, I urge you to deal with your gender issues directly, and don't waste your time and impact the lives of others by trying to be something that you cannot be. However this advice is very difficult to follow, and many people find themselves with spouses and families by the time it becomes impossible for them to continue to live in denial of their gender issues.

Coming out when married is often a particularly bad situation because the trans person may have been concealing his feelings and even cross-dressing activities for a number of years before they are revealed to the spouse. Thus the revelation of your transgenderism is bound to be fraught with feelings of mistrust and betrayal.

Here are some of the worries that are likely to go through your wife's mind when she learns about your gender confusion:

♥ You don't love her.

♥ She isn't pretty enough or sexy enough for you.

♥ If the children find out, it will psychologically damage them.

♥ She will be a laughingstock when her family and friends find out.

♥ You are having extramarital sex.

♥ You will want sex with a man

♥ You will get HIV/AIDS.

♥ You will leave her and she will spend the rest of her life alone.

Here are some of the things she will probably think about what you are going through:

♥ You are nuts. There is no way you are a woman.

♥ This is just a phase; you are going through a mid-life crisis.

♥ You don't really want to be a woman; you just want to play with the fun parts of being a girl.

♥ You have no idea what it really means to be a woman.

♥ You are being terribly selfish. You are not thinking about her or the children at all.

It is no use denying her feelings about these things. You cannot persuade her with logical arguments. These things need to be worked through persistently and lovingly over time. Elisabeth Kubler-Ross's *The Five Stages of Grief* is a good model of how she may need to work through her feelings. You may pass through these stages yourself, either in sync with your spouse or separately.

1. *Denial.* You've probably been in denial for a long time. That's why you got married in the first place—to deny your gender problems and try to make them go away. Finally you emerged from denial and at some point you came out to your spouse. She may go through her own denial stage for a while. Why shouldn't she? It worked

for you for a long time, didn't it? Even before you came out to your spouse, she may well have known that something was going on, but she may have been in denial about it. When you do begin to share with her what you are going through, she may continue to deny it to herself. For example, I had a six year relationship with a woman who was very dear to me. Before we moved in together, I told her I was a cross-dresser. She didn't want to have anything to do with it, so I kept in the closet. One fateful day we had one of those dreadful "getting caught" occurrences. She came home unexpectedly, a day early from a trip to Japan. When she walked into the house, I was in full femme mode. "I told you I was a cross-dresser!" I whined. But she told me she had been in denial about it; she had refused to believe I was serious about it. Six months later she left me. (I was devastated at the time, but in retrospect, I believe she did the right thing and I am grateful for it.)

2. *Anger, resentment.* "Hell hath no fury like a woman scorned," goes the old adage, and the wife of a transsexual is apt to feel scorned indeed. Not only is your wife likely to be angry about your gender issues and that you concealed them from her for so long, but she will probably start to blame it for every problem in your relationship, large and small alike. *"Oh, you think you don't need to take out the garbage now because you are a woman?" "Some woman you are, you still leave the toilet seat up!" "So that's why our sex life is lousy, you want to make love to men!"*

While your wife, and possibly you, too, are in the anger phase, it is the worst time to go through a divorce. Things will be done out of acrimony and revenge rather than striving for the best possible win-win situation. Children will be hurt unnecessarily.

3. *Bargaining.* It may be quite healthy and useful to negotiate the parameters of your transgender activities, as it is with many other aspects of your marital relationship. Just be careful that neither of you are under the illusion that you can bargain the problem away. A typical trap that many fall into is to say, "If we agree that I can cross-dress now and then, I promise that that is as far as it will go." Later when the gender discomfort becomes too much to bear and you decide that you need to do more, your wife will feel betrayed all over again.

4. *Depression.* After the anger has burnt itself out and bargaining has failed to make the problem go away, depression may set it. A doctor may prescribe drugs such as Prozac or Zoloft to help your spouse and/or you through this period.

5. *Acceptance.* You want to get to the point where your spouse can say, "I see that you need to do this and I will support you even though it hurts me." Remember, there is joy at the end of all this for you—your gender dysphoria is cured. For her, there may be no joy. You will no longer be the man she married (although truthfully, he never really existed, except as a mask you wore and an

imaginary model she made up and believed). However, if things go well, there may be joy for both of you in a new relationship as women friends, either platonic or intimate; and she may begin to discover new potentials and possibilities for growth in her own life as well—with or without you.

Relationship outcomes

Every relationship is unique. How your relationship with your spouse turns out depends upon what you both want, separately and together; on how hard you are willing to work for it; and the sacrifices you are willing to make. Here are some typical outcomes that you can consider as models:

♥ *Ugly divorce.* All too often, marriages end up in ugly divorces when a spouse changes sex. It takes a lot of maturity and hard work from both spouses to prevent this most undesirable outcome. Support from family and friends can help a lot, too—but it may be hard to come by. In the ugly divorce, the children may be victims and pawns. They may be taught to hate the parent who "abandoned" them. The trans parent may not be allowed partial custody or even visitation rights, or only allowed humiliating supervised visitation rights, despite a heartfelt desire to continue to be a good parent to the children. In an ugly divorce, nobody wins. Of course, the same is true of any ugly divorce, even if there are no gender issues involved.

♥ *Friendly divorce.* Perhaps one of the most positive outcomes when a spouse changes sex is a friendly divorce. The marriage is dissolved but the couple remains friendly and the parents share custody of the children. I know several trans women whose ex-wives are now their best girlfriends. Getting to this point is rarely easy. There may be a period of one to many years when everybody is in a great deal of pain and there is a huge amount of acrimony and recrimination flying around. Keep your eye on the prize!

♥ *Stay together.* Sometimes a couple stays together despite a spouse's sex change. A fictionalized but realistic account of this type of outcome was illustrated in the 2003 HBO movie *Normal*. Relationships may become even richer and more fulfilling for the whole family after a sex change, because the trans person no longer fights the demon of his gender dysphoria and can be a more loving and open person. Often the subsequent relationship is sexless because the wife "is not lesbian." Other times… well, who knows what goes on behind closed doors? Even non-lesbian women sometimes magically find a strong sexual attraction for one particular woman, and sometimes that particular woman may happen to be their trans husband. Even if the couple decides on separate bedrooms, it does not necessarily mean that they need to lead sexless lives; they may agree to seek sexual satisfaction separately, outside of the marriage bed.

♥ *Stay together temporarily.* Sometimes a couple agrees to

stay together until the children are "old enough." *"Old enough" for what?,* I always wonder. I suppose this might make sense if the kids will be off to college in a year or two, but I don't know about it when the planning horizon is ten or fifteen years. I have more to say on this topic below.

♥ *Negotiated trans time.* Many male cross-dressers dream of having a wife or girlfriend who accepts their cross-dressing and even participates in it. This actually does happen from time to time. For it to be sustainable, the couple usually negotiates boundaries of how much and what type of trans activities will be tolerated. This may be expressed like, "My wife lets me go out dressed once a week, but I can't have any sex!" Hearing this sort of thing always irritates me because adults don't need permission for their actions. However, I realize that it is really just a shorthand way of saying, "My wife and I have maturely agreed that these particular activities are acceptable to both of us."

Negotiating the parameters of trans activities may be workable for cross-dressers, but it is not a long term solution for transsexuals who need to change their sexes and live full time in their new gender roles. It may, however, be a useful tool during a transition period while the family adjusts to the new reality in their lives.

♥ *Willful ignorance.* If the trans person's activities are not full time, he may be able to carry on without the spouse and children knowing about it. But spouses are smart, you know? Children, too. In some cases the spouse and/or the children may be cognizant but willfully ignorant of what the trans person is doing during their frequent nights out or trips out of town. By maintaining a kind of "don't ask, don't tell" policy, they are relieved of the burden of hearing about something they don't want to know about, and they aren't asked to give their approval. This is occasionally a successful long-term arrangement for cross-dressers or other part-time trans people. I suppose it can be healthy as long as the trans person adopts it out of consideration for the feelings of the others; but it is not healthy if the trans person adopts it out of shame. I can't say I personally endorse the "don't ask, don't tell" policy (either in relationships or in the U.S. Military), but it is an option that seems to work for some.

♥ *Death.* I hate to say it, but the suicide rate in the trans community is quite high. I beg of you, avoid this outcome at all costs. As is often said, suicide is a permanent solution to a temporary problem. It is certainly a horrible burden to place on your children. If anyone tells you that you would be better off dead than to change your sex, don't believe them. I am living proof!

One of the saddest stories I heard about a relationship went like this: A trans woman confided that she was feeling terribly guilty. Her wife had supported her through her sex change. Together they had weathered great pain and turmoil, but they kept the relationship intact, and it seemed to be working. But now, a year after sex reassignment surgery, the trans woman felt that the relationship was inhibiting her further growth; she was feeling a need to spread her wings and explore new sexual avenues and relationship possibilities. What to do? I never heard what happened next, but I think there is a lesson here. If you are going to work very hard to preserve your relationship, are you sure that is the outcome you really want?

Something else that happens from time to time is the surprise delayed reaction. It may seem that all is going well with your relationship. You wife has managed to understand and go along with your transition. Then one day, seemingly out of the blue, she announces, "I've decided this isn't what I want for my life. I want a divorce." A visit to trannie-land can be tolerable or even enjoyable, but the prospect of spending the rest of your life there can be another matter entirely. There is really nothing you can do to prevent this from happening; it is your wife's right to make this choice. But if this does happen to you, at least you know you're not the only one to experience it.

Ironically, or perhaps pathetically, when a couple breaks up because the husband changes sex, both husband and wife often wind up in more or less the same situation: they are both middle-aged, single women, each trying to find a good man. This is never easy (but having to explain to your new beau about your sex change makes it even trickier).

If you do wind up breaking up, do not be surprised if your ex-wife's next boyfriend turns out to be a cross-dresser or transsexual as well. I've seen this happen many times, and it often surprises the ex-wife as much as anybody. But, after all, there was something about you that she found attractive in the first place, wasn't there?

Supporting your spouse

Whether a man tells his wife he is really a woman inside and that he's going to change his sex, or if he just tells her that he likes wearing women's clothes, the wife is bound to be devastated. The very foundation of her world crumbles underneath her feet. She thought she was married to a "normal" man; now she finds that she is married to—what, exactly? She "knows" you are not a woman, because she would have been able to tell. Even if you told her you are just a cross-dresser, she will be terrified that you are going to change your sex and leave her.

Here are some things to think about to make it easier on your spouse:

1. Honesty is the best policy. Tell her early and tell her often about your gender issues. If she stays in denial, the relationship will never get to a good resolution. With others, like your parents and children, it may be wise to wait until you know exactly what is going on with you and how you are going to deal with it before you open up to them. With your spouse, this isn't really an option. She is too close to you, and too greatly invested in the outcome. It would be best to discuss your feelings before marriage, but if that didn't happen, you need to come

clean as soon as possible. The longer you wait, the greater her feelings of betrayal and sense of being used and lied to will be.

2. Give her a lot of love and attention. This may prove almost impossible sometimes, especially if you aren't actually feeling that you love her. Maybe her anger and blame are making you feel unloved; maybe you feel that no one ever knew or loved the real you, since you were only showing them a mask until now. It is impossible to truly love unless that love is reciprocated. It is a give and take; both people must feel loved for it to work. But you can always be honest about your feelings; you can still care and be considerate; you can demonstrate that you want to rebuild a loving relationship. Spend time with her. Go to therapy. Talk, talk, and talk some more. Be honest and open. True intimacy is based on really knowing the other person. By trusting her with the truth you demonstrate the desire to truly be intimate with her. Don't focus only on your gender issues; both of you will have other issues unrelated to gender; pay attention to them as well. Work to resolve other things that may be affecting her. For example, perhaps she feels trapped in her job, or in the house. Maybe she'd like to change careers or go back to school. Talk about her hopes and dreams, and make some changes to support them. Don't put all of your family's resources and energy only into fulfilling your own dreams.

3. Don't displace your wife with your new trans girlfriends. It's tempting to become best friends with one or more of

the people you meet in the trans community because they "get it" about the thing that is the big issue in your life right now. But that is the only thing they get about you, and they probably don't even understand that; they're just projecting their own issues. Don't forget all those things your wife does understand about you, and the common history you share together.

4. Reassure her that you will do your very best for her and the children, even while you do what is necessary to deal with your problem. Try to avoid the "ugly divorce," which would make this impossible. If staying together isn't going to work out, try to at least be friends and split up as gently as possible. Your spouse may try to make things ugly out of anger or fear. Try not to fall into the anger trap yourself; respond to anger with patience and understanding if you can. Anger will only damage you and your children. (Don't just deny your anger, but find another outlet for it, like on the racquetball court or in meaningless sex with strangers.)

5. Reassure her that it is not her fault. Tell her that you still find her attractive and sexually desirable. This is just something inside you that you need to do. (Of course, if you don't find her sexually desirable, don't tell her that you do. See item #1 above, "Honesty.")

6. There should be no guilt or shame on either side. It may seem that she wants you to feel guilty, but, if you are honest with her and responsible about your familial obligations, you have nothing to feel guilty about.

Moreover, feeling guilty will not help her in the long run. It only focuses the discussion fruitlessly on right and wrong rather than productively on, "How are we going to handle this?"

7. Don't expect to persuade her with logic. This is not to imply that women are irrational. It's just that there is a huge amount of emotional baggage involved, and it cannot be carted away on a trolley of logical argument.

8. Don't help yourself to her clothes or cosmetics. She will likely feel violated and angry when it comes to light later —and it always will. Women struggle with their self images, and the thought of you wearing her clothes, and perhaps looking better in them than she does, can really hurt.

9. Don't try to force her to accept your issues faster than she can absorb them. This may be easier said than done, but it can be crucially important in keeping the relationship together. Having gotten the "Aha!", you may feel in a huge rush to progress on your transition as quickly as possible; but your spouse may need to take things more slowly. One wife said she felt like her husband was zooming along in a fighter jet while she was peddling along behind on a little tricycle. While this is understandable, it can devastate a relationship. Time can play big role in saving a relationship. One, it shows you care, that you are putting her needs before yours. Two, it allows both of you to resolve other emotional baggage, unrelated to gender issues, with which the

relationship may be burdened. Three, it gives her a chance to adjust. Time can smooth over a lot of hurt, allowing her to complete the stages of grief and get used to the new situation and reality.

10. Don't fight her. If she tells you that you are being incredibly selfish, just accept it. That's how it seems to her. Try not to feel blamed, guilty, or that she is attacking you, even if it seems that way. Try to understand that she is expressing how she feels, and feelings are never right or wrong; they just are. The alternative is a death-spiral of negative emotions. If you don't understand the dynamics of this sort of thing, you haven't done enough therapy yet.

11. Encourage her to seek external counsel—preferably professional. (Her mother is not apt to be very helpful in this situation.) Even insist on it. Offer to go to couples counseling with her. You will likely need three separate therapists, one for you, one for your wife, and one for couples counseling, because otherwise the therapist can be seen to be taking sides. You may even need yet another therapist for the children.

12. Invite her to share your activities, like going to a trans support group or out to a club where you meet other trans friends. But don't try to force her; it's her choice if she cares to participate. If she does go out with you, don't leave her on her own while you hang out with your trans

friends. Make her the focus of your attention—believe me, most of your trans friends will be jealous!

On a related note, don't pressure your wife into participating in your sexual fantasies while are you are dressed en femme. Doing so can be very painful and demeaning to a woman. If you cannot enjoy sex unless you are dressed up, maybe that's something to work on in your therapist's office rather than in your marriage bed. Pressuring your wife into doing something with which she isn't comfortable will be very bad in the long run. Remember that she may be feeling that your gender issues are somehow her fault because she is not attractive enough or not fulfilling your needs; thus she may feel pressured into performing as you wish, while not feeling good about it—even if you don't intend to pressure her.

13. See if any of your trans friends have spouses that would like to talk to your wife. There are precious few support groups for spouses of transsexuals, but they surely need support too.

14. If you are going through a "princess" phase, getting all excited about how cute and sexy you can dress up, don't be surprised if you wife doesn't share your enthusiasm. It's been a long time since she was a teenager, and that's what you're acting like. If fact, she may be quite uncomfortable with such behavior on your part. Women often feel like objects, not valued as real people but only for their sex appeal. By portraying yourself as a sex object you

reinforce this concept, which is one they have probably struggled against for years. The slut/tramp look will often offend a woman who has worked hard to overcome that stereotype and become a mature, real person, valued as more than just a sex object. (Whereas you, who have never before been valued as a sex object, may be very turned on by it!)

15. Show your wife that you are truly interested in being a complete woman, and not just in surfing the fun parts. Pitch in and cook, clean house, and do the shopping, if you don't already do that. Transgender people often focus first on the physical image of being a woman and ignore the emotional aspects: being loving, caring, supportive, and appreciative of the interconnectedness of things. Transitioning through the physical aspects before evolving a feminine emotional framework will make it seem that you are only interested in the shallow physical things. The mental, emotional parts are really the more significant transitions; if you begin to work on those early on, even before your physical transition, it can be a big help to you as well as your spouse.

16. Be willing to shoulder some of the emotional burden. It may give you a clear conscience to be able to say, "I gave it my full support, but she insisted that we break up." But isn't that really just victim consciousness ("I wasn't responsible for what happened to me")? Is the clear conscience worth the price of the relationship? Might it be more honest to say, "Part of me feels like breaking up may be the best thing for us. I'm really unsure about it."?

Also, don't delude yourself; if you know you aren't going to be happy in the existing relationship, be honest about it. Don't make her struggle and work through it only to find out later that it never had a chance of working anyway.

17. Laugh together a lot. You are both going through a very strange experience. It helps a lot if you can laugh at yourselves and at the absurd situations you find yourselves confronting on a regular basis. Also laugh out of pure joy and love, too!

Telling the children

A trans person, and, even more so, the non-trans spouse may be reluctant to tell their children about their transgender issues. I know one cross-dresser who is terrified that his 27 year old son will find out about his cross-dressing. The funny thing is, my friend tells me that his father was also a cross-dresser; and his father's father, as well! I don't have any children of my own (just a kitty) so I can't completely empathize with those who are in this situation. However, I know many who are going through this experience and some of the lessons are quite clear, even to me.

Every parent wants to protect their children from the hurts of the world; but we know we cannot always do that. Good parenting is a delicate balance between protecting our kids from some things and, in other cases, teaching them how to protect themselves and giving them the tools so they can deal effectively with life's difficulties. A parent changing his or her sex is a huge thing, of course; but it is just another one of life's surprises that needs to be handled.

More than anything else, children need love and security. A paramount goal in planning your sex change should be to reassure your children that they are not going to lose you and that you will always love them. Explain this to them and let them help set the parameters for your on-going relationship. For example, involve them in the decision of what they should call you after you transition (many trans women are still called "Dad" by their children, while others become "Auntie").

If possible, do not bring your children into the situation until you are very sure of the path you are on. If you are uncertain about what you are doing and why you are doing it, it will be even more confusing for your children.

Be honest with your kids. They are very sensitive truth-detectors; if you think you can fool them about what is going on, you're probably only fooling yourself. That does not, however, mean that you need to tell them everything all the time. "That is none of your business," is an honest and sufficient answer to many questions.

Take things slowly with your children. Give them plenty of time to get used to the idea, and to see you change gradually.

Children take their cues from their parents. If Mom and Dad are rational and accepting about Dad's transition, chances are the kids will be, too. On the other hand, if Mom is very angry at Dad and feels betrayed, the kids are likely to echo this feeling. Mom, do you want your daughter to hate and resent her father for the rest of her life? If possible, it may be best to wait until you have reached the "acceptance" stage before letting the children in on the situation. If this is not possible, parents should at least try to let the children see them dealing with their anger, depression, etc., in a healthy way, that is, without blaming, guilt, or victim consciousness. This is a situation where doing something—trying to be understanding and positive about Dad's transition—for the good of the children can really make a big difference.

Children, especially adult children, may need to work through the stages of grief much like a spouse. But many times children take the news surprisingly well and easily. I've noticed that children who are healthy and happy in their own lives tend to find it easy to accept and support a transitioning parent; whereas, children who are already struggling with issues of their own may react very badly. They see this as one more burden added to their load; indeed, this may provide a convenient target and become the focus of much of the child's anger. The worst hurt I've seen in trans people are those who have been rejected by a child. The good news is that sometimes the child eventually turns around and finds it in is or her heart to accept the parent back into his or her life. Unfortunately, this may take years; in some cases, it never happens.

Parents always talk about the fear that their children will be teased if Daddy starts wearing a dress. From what I hear, this is not nearly as bad of a problem as you might think. It is the 21st century; Generation Y lives with much greater diversity that we baby-boomers experienced. Gays and lesbians, gay and lesbian parents, people of color, people of mixed race and ethnicity, world cultures, hip-hop culture—these are all parts of children's common experience these days. Transgenderism and transsexualism are still far from mainstream, but today's young people are better equipped to deal with even these differences than we were in previous generations. I haven't heard any reports of cases of a child being severely harassed due to a parent's transition.

When is the best time to tell your children? That's a tough one. There is never a good time in a child's life to get this news. When they are young, you may feel they are too young and vulnerable. When they are teenagers, they are too sensitive to what their friends will say. When they are in college, they have too many other pressures to deal with. When they are adults, they will be angry that they weren't told sooner. There is always an excuse why "now" is not a good time. Since there is no good time in the child's life, you should probably be guided by where you are in your transition and in your relationship with your spouse. As I mentioned before, it is great if you can wait until after you and your spouse have worked through the anger and depression, and are dealing with the issue in a rational, productive way. Do talk to your children about it before they hear it from somewhere outside the family, or before they start seeing changes in you from hormones or your presentation, etc. I know some people who put off transition for years, until the children were grown and off to college. If you can do that, fine. I just wonder, if you can be a good parent and a happy and productive person for all those years, why should you ever transition? Another way to look at it is like this: If alcoholism was destroying your life, would you postpone joining Alcoholics Anonymous because it might reveal your problem to your children? Gender dysphoria can be just as destructive as alcoholism; don't you owe it to yourself and your family to start treating it now?

As usual, there are great resources available on the Internet with advice on dealing with your children and your gender issues. One place to start is www.transparentcy.org.

5 Getting healthy

Why do you want to change your sex? I hope your reason is to make your life happier and more productive, to the benefit of your loved ones and friends as well as yourself. (I can't think of any other good reason.) If so, you must know that the foundation of your happiness and productivity must be good health. Besides, once you work out your gender issues, you are going to be so happy and in love with yourself that you will want to live to be 150 years old—that is not unrealistic, given today's advances in medical technology. Don't you want to spend those years feeling and looking good?

This is not a health book, so I won't spend a lot of time on this topic. I'll bet you already know what you need to do to get healthy. If you are like most Americans, the main things you need to do are stop smoking; lose some weight through a nutritious diet and getting some exercise; and cut down on alcohol and drugs if you use them excessively.

If you need some extra encouragement, here are some reasons why getting healthy should be a part of your sex change program:

- ♥ You will like what you see in the mirror a lot more if you are healthy—in both your old and new gender presentations.

- ♥ Other people will find you more attractive, making you more passable in your new gender presentation.

- ♥ Good health will increase your sexual attractiveness as well as your sexual performance and endurance.

- ♥ Imagine a life with no more hangovers and no more stinky cigarette breath!

- ♥ You can spend your money on shoes and cosmetics instead of ciggies and booze.

- ♥ Therapists are unlikely to be willing to work with you on your gender issues if you have drug or alcohol abuse problems; focus and clear thinking are critically important when dealing with gender issues.

- ♥ Surgeons will not be willing to perform sex reassignment surgery on you if you are grossly overweight, because the risk of complications such as blood clots is too high.

- ♥ If/when you get your new genitalia, you can see them without a mirror if you get rid of that pot gut. For those who are going female to male, you don't want to be staring down at a beer belly after you have those double-D's removed!

Stop smoking

Stop smoking! You already know why you should. If you need one more reason, here it is: Your endocrinologist will insist that you stop smoking before she prescribes hormones for you.

Exercise

Other than not smoking, maintaining a healthy weight is the most important factor in living a long and healthy life. Exercise is a necessary part of any weight control program. That doesn't mean that you need to pump iron for hours every day. It just means that a sedentary lifestyle is a shortcut to the morgue. Fifteen minutes or a half hour of vigorous activity two or three times a week is enough to keep your blood circulating.

Why not include some exercise among the new habits you adopt as you change your sex? Here are some activities that can bring fun into your life and help validate your new gender identity, as well as helping to keep you healthy:

- *Walking.* If you do it at the mall it's called "shopping"!

- *Dancing.* Shake a leg at your local disco, or find an underground rave party. Many people who always hated dancing find that they love it when they do it in their new gender presentation, manifesting their true gender identity. Shake that booty, wiggle those hips; get sexy, get sensual; let it all hang out! (Ahem, Miss Thang, please don't let *that* hang out!) In most dance clubs these days, you don't need to wait for somebody to ask you to dance. Just jump out on the floor and do your thing. Don't worry about being too old; I take pride in being the oldest and tallest person at many of the clubs I frequent.

- *Ballroom dancing.* A great way to meet people, and it's usually a drug- and alcohol-free environment.

- *Tennis.* MTFs, you can wear those really cute, tiny tennis skirts!

- *Golf.* Another opportunity to wear cute skirts, and without sweating off all your makeup, like you do with tennis; plus, you get to use the ladies' tees—that should take a few strokes off your game! (...until the hormones sap your upper body strength.)

- *Swimming.* A great low impact exercise; but swimsuits and locker rooms can be a big challenge for people in the process of changing their sex. For MTFs, going to the pool or the beach in your new bikini is a ritual celebration after sex reassignment surgery. Bolder girls with good tucks do it before surgery.

- *Snow skiing.* Be a ski bunny! Ski outfits are awfully cute and can cover up a lot of body problems (however, drinks in the lodge afterwards can be problematic).

- *Stretching or Pilates.* It keeps you limber. You don't need to go out to a class or even change clothes; just do them on the bedroom floor in your PJs.

- *Crunches or sit-ups.* Okay, they're no fun, but I really think you need them to maintain an attractive, flat tummy. I try to do 50 each morning and each evening.

- *Sex!* 'Nuff said.

Many exercise and sport activities involve use of a locker room for changing and showering. This can be a big problem for people who are changing their sexes. It is much worse than the restroom problem because there is a probability of naked bodies—yours as well as others—being seen in locker rooms. My feeling is that I would not use a locker room until I had my genitals changed. That was easy for me, because I am not much of a sports buff. I know of a few t-girls who use ladies' locker rooms even though they have inconsistent genitalia. Their modus operandi is extreme discretion; they are quite passable and they make sure their family jewels are not exposed. Most people avoid locker rooms completely, or they use the locker room that corresponds to their genitalia. Most will adopt the appropriate gender presentation as well, or perhaps an androgynous presentation. I think that adopting a female presentation in a men's locker room, or a male presentation in a women's, is courting trouble and may be hazardous to your health and safety.

How to stop smoking, drinking, and taking drugs

You can stop smoking. You can stop drinking. You can stop taking drugs. It may be very difficult for you to do, but the process is straight-forward:

1. Decide that today will be the last day that you smoke, drink, and take drugs. Have a binge today if you like. Just don't kill yourself.

2. When you wake up the next day, remind yourself that you are not going to smoke, drink or take drugs today. Then do not do any of those things all day long. Or in the evening. Or at night. It would be a good idea to find some other enjoyable and/or productive activity to fill your time.

3. Repeat step 2 every day for the rest of you life.

4. **Do not skip this step; it is very important:** If you fall off the wagon and find yourself having a smoke, a drink, a toke, or a line, do not despair. All is not lost. You are not a bad person. Simply return to step 1 and continue. (Or step 2—it might be a good idea to skip the binge this time.)

    I'm making light of a very difficult and serious process, of course—probably the second hardest thing you'll ever do (the first hardest for people who *don't* change their sex!) Nevertheless, my simple program embodies two important principles of serious recovery programs: take it a day at a time, or an hour at a time, or ten minutes at a time, if need be. The other principle is that you shouldn't get discouraged if you relapse; you can always start stopping again.

    Support groups, therapists, doctors, books, and other aids that can help you when you find quitting to be difficult. They may work for you. Don't be afraid to try them. I am in alcoholism recovery group myself. My doctor also gave me a great incentive to quit drinking when she told me, "If you don't stop drinking, you will need a liver transplant within five years." I do not want a liver transplant! (A transsexual's blessing: "May all your surgeries be elective.")

    Some people manage to taper off their habits instead of going cold turkey, which is to say, quitting abruptly all at once. Other people don't quit completely, but reduce their habit to a light, relatively harmless level. I don't recommend either of those approaches. I don't think they work for most people. Just quit. That's what I did. I understand that it is not an easy thing to do. I would not have been able to quit my drinking if I had not also solved my gender confusion problems; I was too unhappy. You may need to do some things to get happy, too. Be happy, and quit your smoking, drinking and drugs!

Some girls think that smoking looks sexy. (It looks disgusting to me, but to each her own.) If so, use your ciggies or cigars as props or fashion accessories; just don't light them on fire. On a similar note, if you want to blend in with a drinking crowd but you don't want to drink, order a "Coke that looks like a cocktail." Sometimes I order a "Celibate on the Beach;" that's a Sex on the Beach with no booze. (I made it up, so I always need to explain it to my bartender.)

As for druggie crowds, they usually don't care if you simply decline to partake. All the more drugs for them!

6 Therapy

If you want to seriously explore the possibility that you might be transsexual, I strongly recommend that you spend some time with a therapist who has experience with gender issues. Some people are so sure about their condition that they don't need professional help to sort it out. I think that is rare. Even if it is true for you, what is the harm in talking with therapist about it? There is certainly a lot of potential harm if you are wrong!

I understand the reluctance a lot of people feel about going to a therapist. I fought against it myself for a long time. I said to myself, "I'm smart. I'm an adult. The answers all lie within me. Why do I need a therapist?" Eventually I figured out a metaphor that helped me overcome my reluctance. I used to be a computer hardware engineer by trade, and I took a look at how I solved technical problems at work. I would try my best to solve them by myself, but some problems were intractable. When I was ready to give up, I would find someone else with whom to discuss the problem. If possible, I would choose someone with some expertise in the area, but anyone would do in a pinch. More often than not, simply in explaining the problem to the other person, a new approach or even a solution would spring into my mind. If not, the other person would start asking questions, and that would lead to new avenues to explore. Rarely would the other person actually solve the problem himself, but his help could lead me to a solution. I realized that I could use a therapist in exactly the same way. The therapist would not solve my problems. She would be my sounding board, but I would still do most of the work.

You may not think you need a therapist to be your sounding board, but I caution you to be very careful about trying to use your friends for this purpose. A wonderful thing about a good therapist is that she has no other agenda than what is best for you. Friends and loved ones always have agendas of their own, no matter how much they try to be there for you. They always have their own interests to protect and promote; one interest is probably to not have their good friend—you—change, since that would mean they might lose you. Be especially careful about using another transsexual or transgender person as your sounding board, because, frankly, we're all nuts! I exaggerate. But the fact is that we all have our own issues we're working on, and we have a natural tendency to assume that the answers that are right for us will be right for you too. That can be terribly wrong. (Keep that in mind as you consider my advice in this very book.) Actually, I don't think transgender people are any crazier than most other people; we just appear that way because we are openly confronting our problems rather than masking them with denial like most people do.

You can "play a game" with your therapist to get her to agree to your diagnoses and to approve hormones and sex reassignment surgery for you. The game is simple: just read the stories on a handful of transsexual people's Web sites, and then concoct a story for your therapist that makes you seem similar to them. If you do this, I think you are doing your self a big disservice and missing a great opportunity for personal growth and self-improvement. I believe in being totally open and honest with my therapist. I figure I can always accept or reject her advice, but I will only get her best possible advice if I show her my inner truth as best I can. If I didn't feel I was getting good advice from her, I would find a new therapist. (Most therapists will be happy to refer you to a colleague if you ask.)

The urge to game your therapist is understandable. There was a time not so long ago when therapists expected to hear a certain set of symptoms or else they would not approve you for sex reassignment surgery. Today the understanding of gender identity disorder is vastly improved and good therapists understand that transsexual people have a wide range of feelings and experiences. Today being honest with your therapist should not prevent you from obtaining the treatment you need for you gender dysphoria, regardless of the particulars of your story.

No matter how good your therapist is, you need to do the work. Here are some of the key points you need to understand. You probably won't "get it" just by reading them here. A good therapist can help you to "get it."

- ♥ *You need to be healthy before working on your gender issues.* If you've got drug or alcohol problems, or serious psychological problems like depression, paranoia, or schizophrenia, you probably ought to work them out before you start worrying about your gender. This gender stuff is pretty confusing in the best case. You need a clear mind to understand it. On the other hand, your gender issues may be a root cause for certain other mental problems, in which case you would need to work on both things at once. For example, I don't feel that I would have been able to quit my heavy drinking if I hadn't also resolved my gender issues. Your therapist can help you sort it out; but be aware that she may ask you quit drugs or drinking as a precondition for working with you. (Some people, unfortunately, are afflicted with intractable mental or physical health problems. This should not be a bar to clearing the gender issues. For example, transsexual people living with AIDS should be allowed to undergo sex reassignment surgery; although some surgeons decline to serve such patients.)

- ♥ *People have strong convictions about gender and they are very uncomfortable when they are challenged.* When you meet a stranger, the first thing you size up about him or her is whether he or she is a he or a she. For some reason it is very important to us to know this. No wonder transsexualism is difficult to understand. No wonder you have trouble believing that you might be transsexual.

♥ *Sex is between your legs; gender is between your ears.* As we noted in the first chapter of this book, it is possible for the brain to develop a gender identity that does not correspond to the genitals you had when you are born. This is called Gender Identity Disorder (GID) or transsexuality. It is a relatively rare condition, but not as rare as you might think. Estimates are that one in 250 people are born this way. That's more common than muscular dystrophy, multiple sclerosis, or blindness. Transsexualism is a physical condition, not a mental one. The misery and confusion that transsexualism can bring into your life constitute a mental condition known as gender dysphoria (GD). GD can be alleviated or cured through triadic therapy as laid out in the Standard of Care established by the The Harry Benjamin International Gender Dysphoria Association, Inc. (HBIGDA). Triadic therapy does the best possible job of changing the gender of your body to become consistent with the gender identity in your brain. It consists of transition to living your life in the gender presentation corresponding to the gender identity in your brain; hormone therapy; and sex reassignment surgery (SRS). It is not possible to cure GD by changing the gender identity in your brain, because no one has found a way to do that.

♥ *There is only one you, which has masculine and feminine characteristics.* You may go into therapy like I did, thinking that you have a "boy self" and a "girl self", a sort of split personality. Unless you actually have a split personality (which is to say, Multiple Personality Disorder or Dissociative Identity Disorder, which are very rare, severe mental illnesses), you need to realize that this isn't true. There's only one you. You can take the characteristics which you enjoy on your boy side and those which you enjoy on your girl side, and integrate them into one personality for a fuller, richer life. For example, before I learned this lesson, my "boy mode" was rather pushy, surly, and cynical; also smart and responsible. But in "girl mode" I felt freer to be silly, vulnerable, and sensitive. After I started therapy, I found that I could be a man who was smart, responsible, and sometimes silly, vulnerable, and sensitive; and I could still be pushy when I needed to be. I felt that this was a much more pleasant person to be.

♥ *Nobody has a good definition of what distinguishes the genders.* Ask yourself what makes a woman a woman and a man a man. You can write down a list of qualities like love, caring, sensitivity, assertiveness, strength, and responsibility, but you will quickly realize that none of these qualities are the exclusive province of either gender. You can classify those qualities into the categories of "masculine" and "feminine," but all women and men have a mix of all these qualities, to a greater or lesser degree. It gets very confusing. No wonder people like simply to look at the genitals and be done with it. You will probably arrive at the answer that what makes a woman a woman and a man a man is just that innate feeling of gender identity deep in their psyches. Therefore only you can say what you really are—and you might not be very sure of it yourself, at this point!

♥ *It's okay to be a feminine man or a masculine woman.* Having realized that masculine and feminine qualities can be found in both men and women, it follows that you don't have to change your sex just because you want to indulge certain facets of your true self which seem to go better with the other sex. Are you old enough to remember when nurses and flight attendants were always women? As a society we learned that these "feminine" jobs could be held just as well by men, and it didn't make them any less of men. Likewise, women can be truck drivers, cops, and construction workers, and they're still women. Hooray! You can still be a man and be just as feminine as you please. Or just as masculine a woman as you please. Oh, you may take a lot of abuse for it, and get called "fag" or "lesbo" a lot; you may even get beaten up from time to time. But believe me, that's still easier than changing your sex if your true gender isn't really your problem.

♥ *Your therapist won't tell you whether you are transsexual.* Your true gender identity lies deep in your psyche, and only you can say what it is. Your therapist can suggest ways to look at it and question it, but she won't tell you the answer. In fact, I don't think you will find the answer in therapy at all. As I suggested in Chapter 1, you will find the answer in your real life experience, as you discover which ways of being fit you most comfortably. But the therapist's office is a wonderful place to talk about your experiences and how you feel about them. (Actually, I have heard of cases where therapists have told patients explicitly that they were transsexual. But that's just their opinion, in my opinion; the real answer still must come from you.)

Finding a good therapist

It is critical that you find a therapist who has experience dealing with gender issues. Sad to say, most psychologists do not learn anything about this area in school. Even sadder is that some psychologists do not believe in the legitimacy of transsexualism at all, or they believe it can be cured psychologically. They are simply wrong. If you find yourself in the office of a therapist who tells you that your cross-dressing or gender confusion is sick or that you should use your willpower to quit, thank him or her nicely and find a new therapist.

The best way to find a good therapist is to get a recommendation from another transsexual person, preferably someone who has successfully completed her own transition. Transgender support groups are also a good source of referrals to sympathetic therapists. Some support group Web sites have lists of possible therapists; but of course all information that you find on the Internet should be taken with a grain of salt.

The worst problem in the world

Being born transsexual is a pretty heavy burden, but I would encourage you to try to keep it in perspective. Would you rather have been born blind? Paralyzed? Emilio Estevez? This point came home to me at my first Southern Comfort Conference. One of the lunch speakers was Pauline Mitchell, the mother of Fred Martinez Jr., a 16-year old transgender youth who was murdered in Colorado in June, 2001. As Ms. Mitchell spoke of her son's brief life on the Navajo Indian reservation, it struck me that it is probably easier to be a Caucasian transgender person than a non-transgender American Indian. The horrible bigotry and poverty that Indians endure as a normal way of life is worse than anything I've heard from a t-girl, and no amount of hormones or surgery can bring relief to the suffering Indians. (A lot of compassion and assistance from society and the government could bring great relief to both Indians and transsexual people.)

Here is another example of losing perspective. I met a trans woman who told me, "People won't give me any work because I am transsexual."

"What do you do?" I asked her.

"I do consulting work in mechanical design," she told me.

"How has that industry been doing lately?" I asked.

"Terrible!" she answered. "Nobody can get any work." This was in during the 2001 high tech industry crash.

"Then why do you think the problem is that you are transsexual?" I suggested. "It sounds like your business would be having problems even if you hadn't transitioned." The woman thought about that a moment and admitted it was likely true.

If your transition is causing your marriage to break up, please try to keep that in perspective, too. Divorce is never easy, and it rarely involves gender issues. Hearts are always broken, children are hurt, friends take sides, and finances are ruined. Don't think it is all because of your transsexualism.

Another experience that helped me with perspective had to do with my weight. I was too skinny! I just couldn't seem to put on any weight and I wondered if I might be anorexic. As I researched the problem of anorexia, I was relieved to find that I was not afflicted with this condition myself. But I was shocked to learn just how serious a problem it is. I thought I knew some transsexual people with low self-esteem, but wow!, people battling anorexia can teach us a few things! Not only did I learn about the suffering and struggles of anorexics, but I also became more aware of the criticism and judging of their bodies that girls endure on a constant basis. Maybe missing out on my girlhood has some benefits after all. (A few months later, after I manged to put on twelve pounds, a little, old, gray-haired lady came up to me in a dance club and offered, "Dear, you should wear bulkier clothes. That dress shows off your belly!" That gave me a taste of what I've missed all my life.)

This is not to minimize the difficulty of living with and dealing with transsexualism. We all have our crosses to bear, and transsexualism is a big one. But I would like to remind you to focus on the positives as much as you can, and remember that it is not the worst problem in the world.

In fact, not only is gender dysphoria not the worst problem in the world, but it is also a mistake to think that we transsexuals are the only ones who go through amazing life-altering transitions. Perhaps changing your sex is the greatest change a person can make, but lots of other people go through transformations that re-make their lives in major ways. One that most people are familiar with is becoming a parent . That really changes everything about your life, your self-image, and the way others see you, doesn't it? Here is another example that took me by surprise. When I came out at work, I told my Taiwanese boss that I had been afraid that there might be a cultural problem with acceptance of my transition. He pointed out that he and his fellow expatriates had underwent transitions of their own in leaving Taiwan to come to America; this was a very brave and difficult choice, and often alienated their family back home as well. There are also sadder examples, like those who have crippling accidents or contract debilitating diseases. Divorce is always a heart-rending transition that can rip apart friendships and families. Alcoholics Anonymous has helped transform many lives. I even saw a man on Oprah whose life was changed in surprisingly profound ways when he let the Fab Five from the *Queer Eye for a Straight Guy* television program cut off the long hair and beard he had hidden behind all his life. "I haven't seen my own face in twenty-five years!" he told Oprah, sobbing. So, rather than wallowing in self-pity over the hardships of your transition, try using it as a positive force to connect with other people and empathize with the transitions in their lives.

7 Hormones

Hormones: Magic girly juice for trans women; T for trans men. In both cases it's mainly about testosterone. If you are changing your sex from male to female, you need to get rid of all that nasty testosterone. If you are changing from female to male, you need to get a bunch of it. Hormone therapy is a very serious step. It will produce permanent, irreversible changes in your body.

Hormones are powerful stuff. They are the regulators of all the biological activity in your body. You should only tinker with them under a doctor's care. Your GP (general practitioner) may be able to supervise your hormone therapy, or you may need to see a hormone specialist called an endocrinologist. They will run blood tests before and during hormone administration to carefully monitor the affects of the hormones on your body. The hormones doctors prescribe for MTFs are the same ones used to treat menopause in women and for other medical purposes; but they have not been tested and approved for use in sex changes. The hormones for FTMs are the same anabolic steroids that some athletes use (illegally) to gain muscle mass and discourage fat buildup; again, not tested and approved for sex change purposes. So this is an experimental area of medicine, and constant medical monitoring is imperative for your health and safety. Hormones and herbal hormone precursors are easily obtained over the Internet, and some " do-it-yourselfers" take them without medical supervision. I strongly recommend against this practice; besides the risk of severe complications, how do you know if your dosage is correct and how confident can you even be that you received exactly what you thought you ordered?

Male to female transsexuals usually take two types of hormones, an antiandrogen such as Spironolactone ("spiro" for short) to block the production of testosterone, and estrogen to create a new female hormone balance. Your doctor may start you on spiro for a few months before beginning estrogen. Female to male transsexuals only take one type of hormone, testosterone itself. Hormones may be delivered in pill form, transdermally (i.e., patches), or by injection. Each method has its benefits and drawbacks. Older people, like me, typically use transdermal patches because the drug is not processed through the liver so there is less of a chance of liver damage.

Effects of hormone therapy

What will hormones do for you? It's impossible to say. Individuals have vastly different reactions to hormones. Some t-girls swear that as soon as they popped their first hormone pill, the sun came out, the birds started singing, and all became right with the world. Some say hormones made them feel all girly-like. Others, like me, didn't perceive any immediate reaction. The only psychological changes I noticed were that for a few weeks I was very tense and on edge, like I had consumed too much caffeine, and I had some headaches. I used to joke that I might just as well have drank a lot of Starbucks and hit myself on the head with a mallet! Some trans men say that testosterone made them more aggressive and confident, as you might expect; but other trans men swear that the testosterone had a calming effect on them, perhaps because a testosterone craving in their brains had finally been satisfied.

The Harry Benjamin Standards of Care recommend that hormone therapy should not begin until several months after you have begun living full time in your new gender role; or, it can be started sooner if your therapist recommends it and if you have been in therapy for a reasonable period of time. Most of us start hormones well before going full time. Some therapists, like Russell Reid, the main transgender therapist in Great Britain, like to use hormone therapy as a diagnostic aid. If you go on hormones and it feels good to you, it's a positive indication that you may be transsexual. If it feels wrong to you, maybe you're making a mistake in trying to change your gender. It's a good idea to figure it out pretty quickly, because soon some irreversible changes will start taking place in your body. (Using hormone therapy as a diagnostic tool is another example of the idea I espoused in Chapter 1, that the way to determine if you are transsexual is to try it and see if it feels right to you.)

Over a period of three to six months, hormone therapy will start to produce visible changes in your body. MTFs will experience breast growth, subtle fat redistribution from the belly to the hips and thighs, softening of the skin, and hair becoming more vellus. Unfortunately, hormones will not raise your voice, eliminate your facial and body hair, or produce a nice set of double-D breasts. As a rule of thumb, your breasts will probably grow to about one size smaller than your mother's and sisters' breasts. You should see pretty good breast development in three to six months, but they may keep growing for several years. FTMs' voices become lower in pitch, their facial hair starts growing, and fat redistributes toward the pot gut.

Your doctor will work with you to adjust your dosages to the lowest level needed to trigger the changes in your body's biology. Greater amounts of hormones won't make your breasts grow any larger or more quickly; your body just needs a threshold level of the proper hormones to trigger whatever changes will occur. However, larger dosages may have undesired health consequences, like increasing the likelihood of blood clots or heart problems, so they should be avoided.

Hormones will not turn you gay. Some people think they can, but I haven't found a single doctor or endocrinologist who agrees. What does happen is that female hormones suppress production of testosterone, reducing or eliminating the male sex drive. I think that when a male abruptly finds that he isn't getting turned on by pretty women any more, he thinks he must have turned gay. It's not that; it's just a low libido.

Irreversible changes and long term hormone use

If you decide not to change your sex after hormone-driven changes have taken place in your body, you've got a problem. MTFs will retain their breasts. FTMs will need electrolysis to eliminate their facial hair, and they will need to work on their voices just like MTFs. Your first hormone pill won't produce any irreversible changes, so you needn't fear it; but you'd better have a pretty firm idea of what you're doing if you keep it up for several months. Once you start noticing changes, be aware that they will be permanent. Stop your hormone regimen immediately if you're not comfortable with what you see happening to your body.

Since you, as a transsexual, will be taking hormones for the rest of your life, you may be worried about the recent studies that have cautioned women against long-term hormone replacement therapy (HRT). The current thinking in the transsexual world is, "I don't care, I want my hormones!" Well, that's what a lot of us think. Our doctors have studied the issue more seriously. The HRT results at issue only cover specific HRT formulations, and these typically aren't the ones being used by transsexuals. Besides, as noted before, the application of these HRT drugs for sex change purposes has not been subject to any clinical studies. We are clearly different than menopausal women in many ways, so the results of those studies of menopausal women cannot be assumed to apply equally to our case. In fact, the medical risks involved in sex change surgery itself probably outweighs the risks of menopausal HRT therapies by a large margin. Nevertheless, high doses of hormones can intuitively be assumed to be riskier than low doses. Prudent doctors and endocrinologists encourage their transsexual patients to work with them to minimize the doses they take over the long term. For MTFs, a great way to decrease our hormone requirements is to get rid of those pesky little testosterone generators, our testicles. This done in sex reassignment surgery (SRS), of course. If a t-girl chooses to postpone SRS for a long time, or to forgo it completely, she is encouraged to consider having an orchiectomy, and at least get rid of those nasty testes. Then the antiandrogens can be eliminated from the subject's hormone therapy, and the estrogen can be reduced.

To illustrate how powerful hormones are, let me relate a couple of personal experiences. Some time after my SRS, I complained of a low sex drive and my doctor suggested that

I try adding back a little bit of testosterone. (All women have a low amount of testosterone in their systems, and too low of a level can result in depression and low sex drive.) For me, the testosterone did not improve my sex drive, but it did plunge me into a terrible depression. At first I didn't know what was causing it, but when I stopped taking the testosterone, my depression lifted right away. That made me a believer in the power of hormones. Another time I somehow lost track of the days of the week (this will happen when you are unemployed) and I missed my patch schedule. As a consequence, I had terrible menopausal hot flashes for a couple of days until my body got my hormone levels stabilized again. This taught me to be very careful about my patch schedule—and I suddenly gained a lot of sympathy for menopausal women!

8 Transition

Transition is the word we use to denote the process of changing your sex. You may have already begun your transition by the time you are reading this book. Your transition may not be complete until years after you've undergone sex reassignment surgery, when you finally feel fully and completely at home in your new gender identity and gender presentation. However, "transition" is often used in another sense, to mark the day that you started living full time in your new gender presentation; as in, "Lannie Rose transitioned on January 1, 2002." In this book, I will use "transition" mostly in the latter sense; as shorthand, really, for saying, "began living full time in a new gender presentation."

Transition is the Big Kahuna; it is the brass ring; it is what changing your sex is all about. Forget about sex reassignment surgery (at least until the next chapter). Transition is the point of your sex change: it means to begin living your life as the woman or man you really are inside.

Do not transition unless you absolutely have to. You are very likely to lose family, friends, your job, and maybe even your career. If you are married, it is unlikely that your marriage will survive. A few do, but it is unusual. You will probably lose custody of your children; you may not even get visitation rights. Nobody transitions because it is fun. We transition because it is better than the alternative, which is usually death. I was in the process of drinking myself to death, a sort of slow-motion *Leaving Las Vegas*. (Now I'm a teetotaler. I've been dry for two years. Hooray for me!)

There is no transition schedule that you need to meet. Take your time. Enjoy each step of the process. If you feel that you've pushed yourself too far, drop back a step. Dropping back can be painful and awkward, for example, if you've already started coming to work in your new gender presentation, it will be embarrassing to change back. But what else are you going to do? Keep it up just for appearance sake? That's no good; that's why you started down this path in the first place, to learn to live in a manner in which you are comfortable. Still, it is a good idea to be pretty sure of yourself before you take the next step.

Here are some steps or major milestones for coming out or transitioning.

1. *In the closet.* That's where you'll probably start out, experimenting with your new gender presentation and researching on the Internet in privacy.

2. *Meeting some other transgender people.* You can do this at support groups or at social events or nightclubs.

3. *Going out in public.* You'll want to try your new gender presentation out in normal real life situations, like at restaurants or shopping.

4. *Coming out to your spouse.* If you are married or have a significant other, at some point you will need to let them in on what you are going through. If you think that's going to be tough on you, think of how hard it will be on them. As a rule of thumb, you can expect your spouse's reaction to be very bad. See Chapter 4.

5. *Coming out to friends.* You may want to take some close "straight" friends into your confidence at any point. There is no predicting how any particular person will react to your news. Often their reaction may be the opposite of what you might think. In general, most people seem to find that friends are accepting of them and their news. Almost always, people are surprised, no matter how much you thought they simply must have already known. But now and then you may run into a friend who simply says, "I wondered when you were going to tell me," or, "I wondered when you were going to figure that out!" By far the most common reaction I got from people was, "If

that's what you need to do to be happy, then I am happy for you."

I had three friends that I wanted to come out to, two of my best friends from high school and one of their wives. I thought that the woman would be happy for me; that one friend would be so dismayed that he would put it completely out of his mind; and that my married friend would be disgusted, but he would probably hit on me. (Not that he would "hit me", but that he would try to put some moves on me. I guess I had a pretty high opinion of my appearance.) It turned out that all three of them were fully supportive and happy for me—and they were surprised and a little bit insulted that I had expected negative reactions from them.

If you have gay and lesbian friends, don't expect anything different from them. Most gays and lesbians have no greater familiarity with transgender people than do straight people; nor are they any more likely to be supportive. You might think that they would sympathize with us as downtrodden minorities, but they don't have gender issues, and they don't get why we do.

You can come out to your friends sooner or later, but perhaps later is better. While they may not have any problem with what you are doing, they are not likely to be much help to you in your journey, either. Moreover, you need to be wary of the risk that your friends may accidentally out you to other people who you may not be ready to tell, like family or coworkers.

6. *Coming out to your family.* Sooner or later, the family will have to be told. If possible, make this later... much later. Immediate family—your father, your mother, and your siblings (especially your brothers) are very likely to have big problems with what you are doing. After all, it threatens the whole image of you which they've lived with and by which they've defined themselves all their lives. It's not easy to be told, "Sorry, Dad, but you got it wrong. I'm a girl. Thanks a lot for raising me as a boy." (Please don't say it that way.) Also, if you are uncertain about where you are headed, it will be even more confusing for your family to understand. They will be confused, and only add to your own uncertainly. The best plan, I think, is to get as much as possible of your transition completed before you start trying to explain it to your family. Once hormones start causing visible changes in your body, the cat will be out of the bag and you'll probably need to 'fess up. Your therapist can be a big help in planning this process; she may even rehearse it with you.

7. *Weekend warrior.* You may find that you are spending all day every Saturday and Sunday in your new gender presentation. You are constantly looking for new activities you can do "dressed," whether they are trans-oriented like transgender conferences and parties, or just going out into the real world shopping or going to arts

and crafts festivals. You can't imagine why you would want to spend any time in your old gender presentation, if you have the choice. Or, if you are not out to your spouse yet, you are looking for every opportunity for an out-of-town trip for a week or a weekend where you can spend as much time as possible in your new gender presentation.

8. *Be a 128 girl (or boy).* At some point, you may find that you are a 128 girl or boy: you are living 128 hours a week in your new gender presentation—all but the 40 hours a week you spend at work. Maybe you are also going back to your old gender presentation for visits to the parents or on weekends that you've got custody of the kids. This is a great place to be. You can use this time test your comfort level in your new gender identity in all aspects of your life except at work. My advice is to be a 128 girl as long as you can stand it.

9. *Coming out at work.* When you can't stand pretending you are a boy (or a girl) one more day, then it's time to transition at work. This is a really big deal, because you may lose your job or even your career. For example, professionals like doctors and lawyers may have a very difficult time finding clients who will trust them if they know that they are transsexual. (It's unfair, but think about it this way: Suppose your mother needs a heart transplant, and you can choose between a surgeon who is a transsexual and one who is not. Which surgeon would you choose?) Many transsexual people are chronically

unemployed. On the other hand, maybe it's time for a career change anyway. For my part, I was sick to death of computer engineering, and I was glad to say goodbye to the entire field when I got laid off a year after I transitioned.

Having emphasized the risks involved, let me also say that things aren't as bad as they were a few years or decades ago. Many bosses and companies in many parts of the country and in many industries are very supportive of transsexual workers. They will gladly work with you to support your transition on the job if you are a valuable employee and if you work flexibly with them to make it happen. It is tempting to avoid confronting your current employer; it may seem easier just to quit and try to find a new job somewhere else in your new gender presentation. This is a workable strategy; but I encourage you to give your current employer a chance. What have you got to lose? If it doesn't work out, you can still go somewhere else. Your therapist can help you plan out the best timing and strategy to transition at work.

A final word of encouragement: I found that coming out at work was not nearly as traumatic and embarrassing as I had anticipated. In fact, I felt an overwhelming amount of love and support that I never before sensed was available to me. Afterward, once the fireworks were over and I began coming to work as a woman, I received very little attention and no harassment from anybody. Many trans people have told me similar stories. I wish you similar good fortune in your transition!

10. *Going full time.* If you've transitioned at work, then maybe you are living full time in your new gender presentation. If you are still dressing as a boy when you need to go to the hardware store or to see the mechanic, you are *not* full time! That's fine, there's no law against it —*but*, you'd better not start changing your identification and considering SRS until you are truly comfortable in your new gender identity at all times and in all circumstances. Those who revert to "boy mode" under special circumstances, such as going to PTA meetings or for rich Uncle Howard's funeral, soon find that this is unworkable because everyone starts treating them as women anyway—"boy mode" simply doesn't work any more!

A really *poor* way to come out to anyone with whom you have a close relationship—family, friends, your employer—is to ambush them. By ambush, I mean just showing up at their door in your new femme or masculine presentation, with no forewarning. ("I've got a surprise for you," is not adequate forewarning.) They will be overwhelmed feel very much put on the spot. A much better approach is to explain to them as simply and directly as possible what it is you are going through and what you plan to do. Keep it simple, because their brains will freeze as soon as they hear anything like "sex change" or "transsexual."

This is best done in person, so they can look in your eyes and see your sincerity. If it is not easy to arrange a personal meeting, a phone call or a letter works, too. Be sure to invite them to ask you any questions they might have. Usually the only question they come up with is, "Are you going to have the operation?" Don't be surprised if the other person soon begins to talk about something that is going on in their own lives; your "share" may make them feel comfortable with sharing something of their own—or, it might make them feel so uncomfortable that they just change the subject as quickly as possible. This has happened to me a few times, and I find it annoying. *Jeez,* I think, *what do I have to do to get some attention around here?* On the other hand, I also think, *Whew, at least my news didn't send them into orbit!*

The new you

What are you trying to accomplish with your transition? What do you want the "new you" to be like? I hope your idea isn't to become a Barbie doll or a fairy princess, because dolls and princesses don't get along on their own very well in the real world. As a trans woman, your objective should be to become a real woman, one who likes herself and is able to take care of herself. The object of your transition is to quickly gain the feminization that most women acquire over a period of decades.

You don't have to give up your fishing, woodworking, or watching football. But it could be helpful if you do; it could help to create a more feminine you. Ask yourself, why do you really do these activities? If they are your bliss, by all means keep them. On the other hand, you may discover that you were doing them mostly as a part of your masculine mask, and maybe you will be better off rid of them. For example, for me one of the joys of being a girl is feeling free to just say "No!" to professional sports in all their evil incarnations. Perhaps you might be happier turning your creative energies from woodworking to sewing; investing your home-improvement energies in decorating instead of dry-walling; and exorcising your thrill-seeking needs in daycare instead of skydiving? A room full of toddlers and only you in charge—now there's a truly scary experience!

Don't forget to enjoy the little pleasures of life as you build the new you. Of course you will get your ears pierced (guys as well as gals!); but how about piercing your navel, too? I did. Or your nipples—which I did *not!* Maybe a cute little rose tattoo on your hip, or a nice sexy design down the small of your back? Try a few different hair colors. I never dreamed I would wind up a redhead, but that's what I am today. Get that wiggle in your walk—not just to pass better, but because it feels good and sexy! Paint your toenails—or, better yet, have it done with a full pedicure in a beauty parlor. This is your second chance at life; live a little!

Restrooms, again

When you come out at work, once again you will confront the question of which restroom to use. This time, however, the rules are a little different than they were for public restrooms. For one thing, there is bound to be somebody at work who knows your "secret," even if it is only the Director of Human Resources. Besides the normal modesty concerns, the company may be worried about the possibility of defending themselves in some kind of sexual harassment lawsuit. Another problem is that the company has a right to make policy concerning restroom use, and you can be fired if you violate company policy. OSHA requires that your employer must provide a safe facility for you to use, but they don't say it has to be convenient. Your best approach is to be flexible in working out a reasonable solution with your company's management or HR people. If you are pushy and demanding, it will only encourage them to find a way to get rid of you.

The solution may be simple if there is already a "one-holer" available (a restroom with only a single toilet, for use by one person at a time). If it isn't designated as a unisex facility, maybe it can be changed to one. Often such a facility already exists, equipped for handicapped use. If you agree to use only that restroom there should not be a problem, as there will be no one else in there with you. If a one-holer handicap facility doesn't already exist, the company may be open to installing one.

In most cases you will probably be "out" to the entire company or department. Perhaps some "sensitivity training" sessions may have been held to educate everybody about the issues of transsexualism, to prepare them to deal with your transition. In this case, a good compromise on restrooms is to designate a single restroom, reasonably close to your work area, as the one which you will use. Anybody who has a problem with being in the restroom with you can simply avoid that particular one.

A less desirable solution, but one that has worked for some, is to arrange a signal that indicates when you are in the restroom, or when it is empty. That allows people to avoid the restroom when you are in it if they are uncomfortable with that. Preferably the signal can be something more subtle than a "Caution! Transsexual inside!" sign, but that is the general idea.

What simply does not work is to continue to use the other restroom after you have transitioned. The HR Director at my company told me that the board decided that I should continue to use the men's room after I began coming to work as a woman, until I had the surgery and became a "real woman." This was the first time they had to deal with an employee transitioning, and they were concerned about liability in sexual harassment suits. I said I would try this approach. I used the men's room for several weeks, but it was uncomfortable for me and for the other men with whom I wound up sharing the bathroom. (I never felt that my safety was at risk, but that could be an issue in other workplaces.) I spoke with some of the women in the office about it. They all told me that they thought I should use their facility, so I switched. HR and management turned a blind eye to it, and there was never an issue. I realized I was taking a risk because they could use this defiance of their order to fire me whenever they liked; but I didn't want to ask permission because they might feel compelled to tell me, "No." I guess I was lucky that nobody ever filed a complaint about it. The end of the story is that I was let go a year later in a general layoff, which was fine by me, because I needed some time off for my sex reassignment surgery anyway.

Changing your body

As you transition to a new gender presentation that is consistent with your true inner gender identity, there are a lot of changes you may want to make to bring your body into a form and image that is more consistent with that identity. Here are a list of physical changes for the male to female transsexual person to consider.

1. *Get healthy.* We already did an entire chapter on this topic. You are going through a lot of trouble, pain and expense to change your sex. Why not get your body into its best possible shape at the same time?

2. *Hormones.* As we discussed before, hormones will help grow breasts on the gals and soften their skin; and grow facial hair and lower the voices of guys. Everybody gets some fat redistribution in the directions they want it.

3. *Facial hair removal.* This is the biggest pain, both figuratively as well as literally, that trans women "face." Electrolysis is the only time tested method proven to achieve permanent hair removal. It's the procedure where they stick a needle into the hair follicle and pump it full of heat and electric current until dead; this is repeated follicle by follicle. It hurts, it is slow, and it is expensive.

Most girls schedule a session an hour or two long each week and keep it up for two years or longer. (Q: What do you call 50 hours of electrolysis? A: A good start.) Your electrologist will become one of your best friends.

There are several different electrolysis techniques available. *Galvanic* uses electrical current to cause the formation of lye in the hair follicle, which kills the hair. *Thermolysis* or *flash* electrolysis uses heat for the kill. *Blend* uses a combination of galvanic and thermolysis, galvanic to form lye and heat to increase its effectiveness. Electrolysis can be done with a single probe ("We don't use needles, we use probes!" my operator always chirps—needles are sharpened, probes are not) to work on one hair at a time; or multi-needle, with perhaps sixteen needles being inserted before the juice is applied. Multiple operators can work on you at the same time, if you are in a hurry and you can stand it. All of these methods are effective, and some work better than others for particular people. By "better," I mean less pain, less damage to your skin, perhaps covering more area more quickly, and compatible with your financial situation. Also, be sure to find an operator you like—you'll be spending a lot of time with her! If you are going to be doing five hundred or more hours of electrolysis, you ought to try several different techniques and see what seems to work best for you.

Laser hair removal is a practical alternative to electrolysis for some girls. It still hurts, about the same as electrolysis.

It still takes a year or two, but your sessions are only about ten minutes each every four or five weeks. An entire course of laser treatment may cost $5,000 or so; which may be three times less money than electrolysis. Laser works best if you have dark hair and light skin, and its effectiveness and permanence vary considerably from person to person.

One strategy that is becoming more and more popular is to start with some laser treatments to quickly reduce your overall hair population, and then switch to electrolysis to be sure of a permanent solution.

Until you are well along with your electrolysis or laser hair removal, you will need a good beard cover to hide that five o-clock shadow. I recommend Dermablend Cover Crème, and don't be afraid to trowel it on. I think I personally kept the Dermablend company in business for several years, I was using so much of their product. Another tip is to carry a good battery-operated electric razor like the Seiko Cleancut Shaver in your purse, for quick touch-ups; you can use the shaver right over your makeup, without starting all over from scratch.

4. *Body hair removal.* Electrolysis or laser can also be used to permanently remove undesired hair from other parts of your body—your legs and arms, your chest, your belly, your underarms; even your "bikini region" if you like that look. Your back, too, if you are a poor soul inflicted with hirsutism. Or you can just shave on a regular basis.

Another alternative is to use an epilator, which is a device that uses spinning disks that grab your hairs and rip them out of your skin. It sounds painful, but it's not too bad, except for the first time over an area. I use an epilator on my legs and arms, and I've lasered the rest.

If you are only living part time as a girl, you probably worry about what people will say if you start shaving your arms and legs. Surprisingly, people rarely notice it, or at least they don't say anything about it. I have one cross-dressing friend whose father gave him a bad time about having shaved legs. He made up a cover story that it was because his little son likes to pull his hair. The father calmed down about it after a while.

5. *Ear piercing.* Go ahead and get your ears pierced. It doesn't hurt much, and then you can wear all the fabulously cool earrings. Piercing my ears really helped me feel feminine in the early stages of my transition. Fortunately, a lot of guys have even both ears pierced these days, so you are unlikely to get much hassle for it. Tell your wife that you are going through a mid-life crisis. (She'll have no idea exactly how big a crisis it really is!)

While you're at it, why not get your navel pierced, too? What a great way to show off your new flat tummy, after you've lost all that weight. I did; but I'm glad that I'm old enough that I don't have to pierce anything else. (These kids today, and the things they pierce…)

6. *Fingernails.* Start growing your fingernails out. If you are in boy mode and people notice your long nails, they will just think you are a slob—as long as you don't have them painted! A lot of women have short fingernails, so keeping them short isn't going to hurt you much as far as passing goes. But long, elegant fingernails feel really sexy and feminine. I get compliments on my nails all the time. People can't believe they're real.

   Fake press-on nails look fake and they come off at the worst moments. A good set of acrylics that you get at a beauty parlor or you glue on yourself look great, but you need to get them done every couple of weeks to keep them looking nice, they're very difficult to remove, and over time they ruin your real nails.

7. *And more hair.* Lord, we go through all that trouble removing hair, but then there's never enough on the tops of our heads. Of course you will want a nice feminine hair style. Chances are that your male hair simply won't do, no matter how you style it. Cheap wigs in the $20 to $80 range are fine for starting out, especially for trannie-friendly venues and vampires. If you want to pass in public, invest in a nicer wig, in the $150 range at least, and replace it once a year as it gets ratty. If you are going full time, I think it is worthwhile to invest in an excellent human hair wig or "hair integration system" customized for you especially; this will cost in the range of $1,000 or $1,500.

Nothing is as nice feeling and authentic as your own natural hair, so start growing it out today! It took me a year and a half to grow out my hair to the point where I was comfortable wearing it alone on a regular basis. My $1,500 custom hair integration system still looks nicer than my natural hair, but I only bother with it on special occasions. Hair extensions can be a good bridge between wigs and your natural hair, if your hair isn't long enough yet on its own.

The other nice thing about your natural hair is getting it styled, colored, and perm'd. Go nuts! The beauty parlor is very relaxing, and a great place to build your feminine social skills.

8. *Develop a feminine sounding voice.* Anyone can develop a feminine sounding voice, but it takes a lot of practice and discipline. Often this is the single hardest thing for a t-girl to do. It's not just a matter of pitch; in fact, that is the least of it. It also involves resonance, dynamic range, enunciation, word choice, and even body English. I was lucky to be blessed with a squeaky, high-pitched voice (which was a curse when I thought I was a guy), but I still needed to work on the rest. You might look up Melanie Anne Phillips's *Develop A Female Voice* (http://store.yahoo.com/transgender/devfemvoic1.html) as a place to start. Melanie says you can do it in six months if you work hard at it. Another excellent resource is Andrea James's *Finding Your Female Voice* (www.deepstealth.com/store/). But until you have a

chance to do the hard work, you will be surprised at far you can get simply by speaking in a soft, gentle voice—even soft enough that people need to strain to hear you. But *don't* try to modulate your voice up to a falsetto, like when the Monty Python gang does drag ("Ooh, there's a penguin on the tele!"); that won't fool anybody.

9. *Surgery*. Let's save this topic for the SRS chapter, coming up next.

If you are like me and like most transsexual women and men, you will want to live as much as possible in a totally natural state when all is said and done and your transition is complete. If you can, you will want to wear your natural hair instead of a wig—even if that means using Rogaine or getting extensions. You will not want to be putting "chicken fillets" (don't those silicone breast forms look rather like boneless, skinless chicken breasts?) in your brassiere every day, so get comfortable with the breasts that god and hormones gave you, or get implants. Forget about false eyelashes, fake fingernails, and hip and butt pads. When you are a natural woman or man, you will feel freer and more at home in your body, and that will help you pass better—people will pick up on your authenticity. You will not be trying to "pass" as something you are not; you will, in fact, be the authentic person you truly are.

Changing your name

Finally, there are the mechanics of transition, which mainly consists of changing the name on all of your legal identification documents. Presumably you chose and started using a new name appropriate for your new gender a long time ago. Be sure you like it before you start changing it legally, because you will be stuck with it for the rest of your life. A lot of people, like me, choose a new first name with the same initial as their old name, so that their initials remain the same. I was "Edward," now I am "Elaine." I didn't have to change the monograms on my shirts (although I gave them all to Goodwill anyway), and my e-mail address stayed the same. Sometimes you can sign documents with just a first initial and your last name, like when you get airline tickets (at least, you could do that before 9/11). This trick can ease some phases of your transition.

When I got serious about transitioning, I decided I didn't like "Elaine" very much, because it sounded too stuffy to me. My solution was to keep "Elaine" as my legal name and use it for business purposes, but I asked all my friends to call me by the more casual nickname, "Lannie."

If you have a spouse and children, you may want to choose a gender-ambiguous name like "Pat," "Chris," or "Jamie." That can make it easier for your family to identify you by name without having the subject of your sex come up in certain situations.

You might be wise to avoid the names "Michelle" and "Jennifer." They are obvious choices for Michaels and Johns, but, for that very reason, they are oversubscribed. It is not unusual to find myself in a group of trans women including four or five Michelles and three Jennifers. It's gotten to the point where those names alone are enough to out you. Also, if you are actually changing your sex, eschew the beautiful name Amanda. It may be a great name for a cross-dresser or a drag queen, but no so much for a transsexual. I know a beautiful, young trans girl who was crushed when someone explained to her the implication of her name: "A man, duh!"

Many trans people take a new middle name. I decided to go with no middle name at all, because I am tired of trying to remember when I need to use it and when I don't.

Some trans people choose to change their last name. I felt that I would keep mine, since I am still a member of that family. But if your family disowns you (it happens), or if you want a more complete break from the past, or if you've just got a horrible last name, this is your opportunity to change it.

Getting a court order changing your name is simple; you can do it yourself without a lawyer. Your local municipal court will have the forms and explanations of the procedure, and there are plenty of other resources available to walk you through it. You can also change your name through a process called "common usage," which involves simply using the new name exclusively for five years, but this is rarely done and besides, it's useful to have the copy of the court order in your hands.

Once you have the court order, you'll want to get your name changed on your driver's license and social security card. This is pretty simple to do, although sometimes the two things are interlocked in a Catch-22 manner. Hope that you draw a friendly DMV clerk. Getting the "sex:F" (or "sex:M") on your driver's license is a major milestone in every trans person's life. Celebrate—hooray!

Finally, you need to contact your bank, all your insurance companies, your employer, and everybody who sends you bills, and get them all to change their records. Don't forget your automobile registration and the mortgage on your home. I involved a lawyer with my mortgage change because I wanted to make sure it was done correctly. (We deeded the house over from me as my old name to me as my new name.) Change your voter registration; I changed from Republican to Democrat at the same time. If you're e a young-un, you'd better contact your draft board and let them know what you're doing. You may want to write former employers and your schools and have them change their records, so they can find you when you have references checked when applying for a new job or credit, etc. Colleges will re-issue your degrees in your new name. It's not possible to change your high school yearbook—sorry! But you are a shoo in to win "Most Changed" at your next high school reunion, if that's any consolation.

Most places have very little trouble processing your name and, in a few cases, your gender change. Many times it can be done with a simple phone call. Some places will require a copy of your court order, even a certified copy. You need to grit your teeth and slog through it all. It's easy enough to work through in a couple of months.

You might think that banks and credit cards are your biggest problem. They turned out to be the easiest thing for me. My bank added my femme name as an "AKA" (Also

Known As) on my account, even before I had it legally changed. That way I could do business under either name. They issued me credit, debit, and ATM cards under my new name, and printed up new checks for me. I don't know if all banks will automatically do this for you, but it doesn't hurt to ask. Talk to you personal account representative if you have one, or to a manager otherwise.

You will not be able to change your U.S. passport until you can provide a letter from you doctor asserting that you have had sex reassignment surgery. I guess you're just out of luck if you plan to live without the operation. If you are having your surgery performed overseas, the passport agency will issue you a non-renewable temporary passport in your new gender to use for the trip.

You may want to do a clean sweep by having your birth certificate changed as well. The policies on this vary state by state. Some states will change the certificate; some will only annotate it so that anyone doing research on you will see that you changed it. All states will change your name, but a few will not change your gender. Sorry! I think that all the states that will change your gender currently do so only after sex reassignment surgery. You will need to check on your own state's policies.

♥ ♥ ♥

9 Sex Reassignment Surgery

SRS. Sex reassignment surgery. Getting your permanent bathroom pass. Learning to speak Italian (as in female gen*italian*). Losing the lizard. Removing the remora. Changing your outie to an innie. De-installing your floppy. *The Operation*—as in, "Are you going to have *The Operation?*"

Here is some more good news: You do not need to undergo sex reassignment surgery! Many trans women and trans men do not. They live happily as pre-ops, meaning they have not had a sex change operation but they plan to some day; or as non-ops, meaning that they never intend to have the surgery.

SRS is the procedure that actually changes your genitals from a penis to a vagina or vice-versa. Some people prefer to call the procedure "GRS," which is an acronym for "genital reconstruction surgery;" or "genital reassignment surgery;" or "gender reassignment surgery." Nobody seems to agree on what it means. I like to give it a modern high-tech spin and say "genital repurposing surgery." But usually I just say "SRS," because I have no problem with keeping the "sex" in "transsexuality."

My advice is that you should not worry about SRS at all until after you have transitioned. Once you start living your life in your new gender role, your attitudes about lots of things will change. After you have settled into your new life, that is the time to start considering whether SRS is right for you. In my own case, SRS was pretty far from my mind when I transitioned. After living as a woman for about six months, my penis seemed more and more out of place. That's when I started seriously looking into SRS.

Some trans women feel that SRS is what finally turned them into real women. Many, like me, do not. I like to say, "SRS does not make you a woman any more than rhinoplasty makes you a rhinoceros." I believe I always was a real woman. In a practical sense, I felt my sex was changed once I was living and working full time as a woman and I had legally changed my name. What I had between my legs never came into play in my day to day existence. Nevertheless, I still had a feeling of discomfort about my male genitals being incongruous with my female gender, and I needed the surgery to relieve that discomfort.

Some trans people do feel that SRS was the turning point that actually allowed them to think of themselves as fully a woman or a man. I'm not sure if it is just a semantic difference about what we mean by being a real woman, or that SRS is really more important to them than it was to me. It doesn't matter. Either way, it's okay,

Here are some *bad* reasons for having your genitals surgically modified:

- ♥ Your sex life is lousy now, and you think SRS will make it great.

- ♥ Your sex life is great now, and you think SRS will make it better. Ironically, you may wind up with no sex drive at all, once your testosterone is gone; that's what happened to me.

- ♥ Transition isn't working for you but you think SRS will fix it.

- ♥ All your transsexual friends are doing it.

- ♥ It will really piss off your father. (It will, but still…)

- ♥ You need it to legally change your passport, or to get married, etc. (You do, but still…)

- ♥ You want to make sure that if you get arrested, you get locked up with the women. (What are you doing that's going to get you arrested? Stop that!)

♥ You will look cuter in your bikini.

Here are the *good* reasons to have SRS:

♥ To cure your gender dysphoria.

If you get SRS for any reason other than to alleviate your gender dysphoria, you are bound to be disappointed in the long run. "Disappointed" is too mild a word. People who regret their SRS are absolutely miserable, and often suicidal. Gender identity runs really deep in your psyche, as you must have realized by now. Tinker with it (and flaunt the Harry Benjamin guidelines) at your peril!

Real Life Experience

Did you know that you need to transition at least a year before you are eligible for sex change surgery? It is one of strongest requirements set forth in the Harry Benjamin Standards of Care. This is called your Real Life Experience (RLE) and it confirms your ability and your resolve to live successfully, happily, and productively in your new gender presentation before you take the irreversible step of SRS. Sometimes the term Real Life Test is used, but this is less accurate because it is not a test that you pass or fail; it is an experience to help you decide your best course of action.

Some trans people bridle at the idea of an outside authority policing their life decisions and they circumvent the requirement for RLE. I feel strongly that once you have made the decision to change your sex, you should live with your decision for at least a year before you take serious irrevocable steps like SRS. However, I can appreciate that in some cases this may not meet Harry Benjamin's RLE criteria. Some people have no confusion at all about their gender identity; they know exactly what they are, and they just want to get their genitals fixed. As I see it, these people have lived with the decision to change their physical sex from an early age, so when they actually transition and have surgery is not so important in terms of being sure they are doing the right thing.

Many people begin RLE, that is, they begin living full time in their new gender presentation, and after a month, or three months, or a year, they find that it isn't working out for them. One person may decide that he prefers to live as a man if that means he can stay together with his wife and children, rather than as a woman without them. Maybe another person cannot tolerate being clocked all the time. Someone else may find that it just isn't as fun or fulfilling as he thought it would be, or maybe it's just too much trouble to maintain a feminine presentation. For any of these or other reasons, they return to their previous gender presentations, with their attitudes having been enlightened by their walks on the wild side. There is nothing wrong with this, and no one should hesitate to return to their old self if they are uncomfortable with their new life. This is not an irrevocable change—they can always transition again later on, if they feel the need to. Maybe they simply were not adequately prepared the first time, and the next time it will work out just fine. That is what RLE is for. But once you have the surgery, going back is less easily and less satisfactorily accomplished—much less!

Successfully completing a year or two of RLE does not guarantee that surgery or a permanent sex change is necessarily right for you. One or two years isn't all that long in the context of a lifetime. What matters is not the time, but how you feel about it. If you don't feel that you are ready for surgery, that's okay. Many girls wait five, ten, or even more years before having surgery. Some never do. It's all good—except having surgery and then regretting it. In any case, RLE and the Standards of Care cannot prevent someone who is bound and determined to get SRS from doing it, no matter how bad an idea it might be for them. Ultimately, the responsibility for your decision is yours and yours alone, and you will have to live with the consequences, be they good or bad.

Letters

In addition to RLE, the Standards of Care require that you produce two approval letters; one must be from a psychiatrist and the other can be from your therapist. These health professionals are *not* certifying that you are transsexual. Only you can determine that. They are saying that they don't believe you have any other mental conditions that prevent you from properly and responsibly making that determination; and that they think your transition is going successfully as far as they can observe.

Are you ready?

Here are some thoughts, half serious, about whether you may be ready for SRS:

- ♥ If you brag about how big your penis is, you may not be ready for SRS. (Girls that are ready for SRS brag about how *small* their penises are.)

- ♥ If you still pee standing up, you may not be ready for SRS.

- ♥ If the thought of SRS gives you the creeps, you may not be ready for SRS.

- ♥ If you have no concerns about the risks and pain of SRS, you are not ready yet. Do some more research, and make a realistic decision.

- ♥ If you don't have the cash money to pay for SRS, you are most certainly not ready for it! (Some girls have been known to finance their SRS by borrowing on their credit cards and later, after the surgery, declaring bankruptcy. I can't say that I really recommend this approach; it takes years to repair your credit rating. Besides, is that really the way you want to begin your new life of being totally honest with your true self?)

Are you ready to go ahead with your SRS? Okay, but there's one last detail before we do it. You may want to consider banking some sperm or eggs. Once your surgery is done, your procreation options are severely limited. Many trans women bank sperm so they can later create genetic offspring with a female partner or surrogate mother; and likewise trans men may bank their eggs.

The surgeries

There are a variety of surgeries that may be involved in changing your sex. SRS for the MTF itself is a collection of these surgical procedures:

1. *Penectomy.* Dissection of the penis, preserving some parts (the skin is used in the vaginal canal; the nerves and glans are preserved to create the clitoris; and the urethra tube is rerouted for urination).

2. *Orchiectomy.* Removal of the testicles.

3. *Vaginoplasty.* Creation of the vaginal canal using the penile skin plus skin from the scrotum, or a skin graft, or a section of colon.

4. *Clitoroplasty.* Creation of the clitoris from the penis glans tissue and nerve bundle.

5. *Labiaplasty.* Creation of the labia majora and labia minora from scrotal skin.

When all is said and done and you are all healed up, you should quite pleased with the cosmetic appearance of you new vulva. You don't need to worry about the Hedwig effect ("The Angry Inch"). Many girls laugh about how a gynecologist remarked to them, "My, you've had an excellent hysterectomy," not being able to tell that their vaginas were anything other than natural. Oh yes, there are some horror stories out there. Dr. Schrang has a number of them in his famous slide show. But the top surgeons are producing excellent results on a regular basis these days. And pretty much any result is better than that thing that used to hang there before, isn't it? (If you don't answer "Yes" to that one, maybe you should think harder about your desire for SRS.)

Poor trans guys! FTM "bottom surgery" to create a phallus is much more complex, painful, and expensive than MTF bottom surgery; and, unfortunately, it yields much less satisfactory results even in the best case. For this reason, many MTFs forgo bottom surgery. On the other hand, "top surgery", a double mastectomy, may be of as great importance to the trans man as bottom surgery is to the trans woman. In both cases, the procedures remove undesired "extra" features which must otherwise be bound and concealed, often painfully.

MTF SRS in 2004 costs around $7,000 if done in Thailand (including travel, room, and board); it's about two or three times as much if done in North America. The prices go up a little every year, and certain Thai surgeons seem to be hiking their fees to be closer to those of their western counterparts. FTM SRS can run $80,000 or more. Usually the patient must pay these expenses out of her or his own pocket and up front, as most medical insurance policies classify this surgery as "experimental" or "elective" and they will not cover it. San Francisco city employees and Canadian citizens are in better shape; their health insurance covers sex change expenses. Some lucky folks have been known to talk their insurance companies into covering it, so you might want to give it a try. It may help if your doctors are willing to be creative about how they specify their diagnoses.

I thought that the most common question people would ask me about my surgery would be, "Do you have any regrets?" (Answer: *No!*) But it turns out that there is something else that people wonder about: What happens to the leftover parts? One girl who was planning her SRS joked that she wanted to keep them on her mantlepiece in jar of formaldehyde to freak out her friends. I am sorry to say that the hospital won't return your parts to you; they are sent to the lab for biopsy to check for the presence of cancerous cells or other possible problems. (That girl decided she would put a Jimmy Dean sausage and two pickled quail's eggs on her mantlepiece, and if her friends weren't sufficiently freaked out, she would pull out one of the eggs and eat it!)

...And more surgeries

SRS isn't the only surgery involved in changing your sex. Trans women may undergo facial feminization surgery (FFS) to make the features of the their face more passable. Some girls choose to have FFS just prior to beginning RLE because they feel it is critical to help them pass as a woman in their day to day life.

Depending on you own needs, desires, and pocketbook, you can choose from a menu of FFS procedures includes brow shave, rhinoplasty, jaw reduction, chin implants, and other items. A scalp advance can help overcome a receding hairline coming from male pattern baldness (other approaches include hair plugs and Rogaine/Minoxidil). A trachea shave to eliminate the tell-tale Adams apple is very common. Some girls spend $20,000 to $40,000 on FFS procedures.

I think you should only consider FFS if you have particularly masculine features and are having a difficult time passing in most circumstances. Although FFS is startlingly effective in feminizing the face, it only creates confusion if you wind up with a feminine-looking face on top of a linebacker's body; or very feminine features on a face that's still too damn large. (Men's faces are larger than women's—haven't you noticed that?) In my case, I just had a nose job. Despite my reservations, I have to admit that every girl I know who has had more extensive FFS has been very pleased with her results.

Surprisingly, no approval letters are required for FFS like they are for SRS, even though FFS is irreversible and makes a profound difference in your physical appearance. Should you be one of the unfortunate few who tragically decide they've made a terrible mistake and they "untransition" back to their original gender, FFS is probably a bigger problem than SRS since everybody sees your face every day.

The surgical options for your sex change do not stop at SRS and FFS. Of course many women—trans and non-trans alike—elect to have breast implants to improve their bust line. One survey indicated that about half of all trans women do it. Trans women are advised to let the magic girly juice (hormones) work their magic on their breasts for at least a year, better yet two or three years, before getting implants. Your natural growth may provide all the mass you feel you need. Besides the gradual growth you would anticipate after you start on hormones, unexpected growth spurts have been reported after SRS and even many years after regular hormone use. In addition to size considerations, the growth will also change the shape of your breasts; so if you get implants too soon, you may be delighted right after the surgery but you may not like the shape of your breasts a year or two later. Nevertheless, a lot of girls have breast implants done as part of their SRS surgery. This adds a lot more pain to the recovery period; in fact, some girls say that the top part hurt a lot more than the bottom part. This is because of the stretching of the muscle tissue to make room for the implants. But everyone I know who had implants is absolutely delighted with their results.

Some "doctors" offer silicone injections to increase breast size, add some womanly padding to the hips, and to smooth out facial wrinkles. This practice seems to be most common in Mexico and South America. Often the practitioners are not doctors at all. Injections of liquid silicone are a horrible idea. Unlike breast implants, where the silicone (or, more typically, saline) is encapsulated in a rubber membrane, injectables are unconstrained and will migrate throughout the body and cause terrible health problems and deformations. Don't let anybody who is not a licensed, reputable doctor, or a nurse working under a doctor's direction, inject you with anything! (Diabetics, you may inject your insulin. You know what I mean.) Stay away from silicone injections under all circumstances.

Some trans (as well as non-trans) women elect to have liposuction to eliminate some of their fatty deposits. Be aware that this is usually only a temporary measure; you will store more fat back in those same places in a year or two. Trans (as well as non-trans) men don't have this problem; they just get fat and no one cares.

Some girls have surgery to help make their voices sound more feminine. To my understanding, such surgery is not consistently successful, and may leave your voice in worse shape that it was originally. Anyone should be able to develop a feminine sounding voice without surgery, as I mentioned in the Chapter 8. It's up to you if you want to try the surgical option; but I I urge you to approach this (and all surgeries) cautiously.

The downside of SRS

SRS is not all fun and games. Come to think of it, very little of it is. We love the results, but getting there takes a lot of pain and inconvenience. Here are some of the unpleasant aspects of SRS; don't say I didn't warn you!

1. *Scrotal electrolysis.* Some surgeons advise you to have electrolysis done on your scrotal skin prior to surgery. The scrotal skin will be used to construct the interior wall of the neovagina, and one does not want hair growing deep inside one's vagina. Some surgeons prefer to remove the hair follicles from the scrotal skin by other methods during the SRS procedure, so be sure to ask your surgeon what he wants you to do. My surgeon, Dr. Annette Cholon in Menlo Park, California, lined my vagina with a skin graft taken from my thigh rather than scrotal tissue, so scrotal electrolysis was not an issue. That is one of the reasons why I selected her!

2. *Risk of surgical complications.* I don't think I need to belabor the point that SRS is a major, invasive surgical procedure. Like any such procedure, it carries a risk that something will go wrong, such as infection, hemorrhage, fistula, etc. Fortunately the risk of serious difficulties is small these days, provided you go to an experienced, reputable surgeon *and* you follow your various doctors' and surgeons' orders and advice, both pre- and post-surgery. On the other hand, be aware that the chance of a minor complication or two is highly likely, but usually

easily remedied. For instance I had excessive bleeding that required a second trip to the OR three days after my initial surgery. (This was at least medium on the scale of minor complications.)

3. *Pain.* The next thing you should realize is that SRS hurts! The amount and duration of the pain varies from person to person, but in any case SRS is no walk in the park. Morphine is indeed a wonderful pain-killer, but its own side-effects become miserable after a day or two. The pain directly from the surgical site is not so bad, but your whole body is debilitated for a period of time. Some girls are up and shopping or literally taking walks in the park in three days. In my own case, it was a couple of weeks before I felt strong enough to go out.

4. *Catheter.* You will be tubed-up to a urine bag for at least a few days. I had my catheter in for ten days, including several days after I left the hospital. Once I got past the "Ewwww!" factor of having a urine bag as a constant companion and fashion accessory I actually got to like it, because I didn't have to worry about when to pee. By the way, it did not hurt at all when the catheter was removed.

5. *Follow-up surgeries.* Even if you, like me, have a so-called "one-step" procedure, where the labia majora and labia minora are created at the same time as the intial penectomy/vaginoplasty, it is not unusual to need a little bit of follow-up surgery. In my case, we did this to create

the clitoral hood and remove some excess mucosal tissue. This was not a big deal, just an office visit under local anesthesia. Other girls have told me of one to several procedures to re-position the urethra to fix peeing problems (see below). Some surgeons prefer to do labiaplasty as a separate procedure about six months after the initial operation; so we call that a "two-step" procedure. Prior to my surgery it seemed important to me have a one-step procedure; but at this point, anything that doesn't require full anesthesia is little bother to me.

6. *Additional costs.* Your follow-up surgeries and general follow-up care (office visits for check-ups) may add to your SRS expenses. In my case, my surgeon's initial fee included any follow-up surgery as well as office visits, so that worked out nicely for me. I was required to cover additional costs such as hospital and operating room charges and anesthesiologists for unplanned follow-up surgeries. I incurred some such charges for that surprise second trip to the OR that I took three days after my initial SRS. Much to my surprise, my medical insurance helped out on those bills. So there's an idea: try billing your insurance even if they've got a policy against covering SRS-related charges. Also, if you are on a tight budget, don't forget the costs of supplies such as lubricating jelly (for dilating, see below), antibacterial soap, Maxi-pads and panty liners, Monistat®, your donut pillow, etc.

7. *Peeing.* Yes, peeing. They will remove several inches of your urethra as well as some or all of your urethral sphincter muscle. It's going to affect the way you urinate. When my catheter was removed, it took me a couple of weeks to develop control of my urination with my new plumbing. By "control" I mean that I was wetting myself before I could get to the toilet. I needed to learn to become alert to the very first tingling signaling time to go, and then to get to a bowl "stat." Over the next few months I became able to "hold it" better and better, so it wasn't necessary to move quite so quickly. But I still need to take care of business faster than when I had that extra length of urethra. Some girls suffer worse incontinence than I did, and for some incontinence and seepage are permanent problems. That means Maxi-pads every day— so much for that smooth silhouette you expected in your bikini bottom! (These problems are not unusual for any women, especially after childbirth and with age. Now you know why bikinis are for young girls.)

8. *Spraying.* And that's not all on the topic of peeing. There's also the issue of impersonating a garden sprinkler. Your water is not likely to exit in the well-mannered stream that you were used to, at least initially. There is going to be a lot of swelling in your various insulted parts, and that will squeeze your urethra so it sprays pretty wildly. Also it may point in the general direction of down your left thigh, or toward your right shoe, or into your face, anywhere but down into the bowl where you want it. Both of these problems are likely to correct themselves

somewhat over the first few weeks and months. After about three months I was fortunate to be able to pee in a compact stream down into the bowl. But it is not unusual to have minor corrective surgeries to fix these types of problems, and some girls have permanent complaints in this embarrassing area. (By the way, the sound of my peeing is now a constant stream like the genetic girls, but not as powerful. I wonder if that will come with time. If you don't know what I'm talking about, I guess you are not using the ladies' restrooms yet.)

9. *Dilation.* After your recover from your SRS, and for the rest of your life, it is necessary that you dilate your neovagina on a regular basis. Dilation prevents your vagina from shrinking and trains your pubococcygeus (PC) muscle to relax. It is accomplished with a set of graduated "stents," which are hard plastic dildos with diameters from an inch to and inch and a half or larger, which you insert into your neovagina. During the period immediately after surgery, dilation takes a tremendous commitment of time and resolve. For a few weeks immediately following surgery, your doctor will instruct you to dilate four to six times a day, for a half hour each session. The frequency of dilation is decreased as time goes on. After six months, you will be down to once a day for an hour, and you will be very grateful for that! You will need to continue to dilate your vagina for the rest of your life, with the frequency decreasing to once every week or two. I am sorry to say that I get absolutely no erotic pleasure from dilating, although some girls say they

do. One bright note: dilation can be replaced by frequent sex.

10. *Infection.* Urinary tract infections (in your urethra) are very serious and painful. They must be treated immediately. These are best avoided by being very careful about keeping your vulva and your equipment such as dilation stents clean and sterile. I have been fortunate to have been spared this problem, at least so far. Then there are yeast infections, which can occur inside the vaginal canal and also externally in the folds of the labia. Be sure to examine you vulva carefully with a hand mirror often, to catch yeast infections as soon as they crop up. I got my first yeast infection a couple of months post-op. "How womanly!" I smiled. Eight weeks later I was grimacing, "Why can't I get rid of this god damn infection??!!!" You should expect to get yeast infections. You will need to work out just the right recipe of washing, drying, and douching to keep them at bay. One girl I know wears a tampon all the time to keep her vagina dry. She swears it is the only way she can avoid yeast infections (though I am not recommending this particular approach). My yeast infection wasn't very itchy or painful, just annoying. The worst thing is that you are not allowed to have sex while you've got a yeast infection because it is transmissible.

11. *Healing time.* We tend to fixate on the magic six week window: six weeks after the procedure, if all went pretty well, your surgeon will release you for all activities, including sex. Hooray! But healing is not complete at that

point. The swelling will continue to go down for six months, just like for a nose job. After about three months, your vulva will be close to its final appearance (barring any subsequent follow-up surgeries). If your surgery is planned as a two-stage with a separate labiaplasty, that will probably happen at about six months. It can take six months to a year for your insulted nerves to get fully set and firing in their new configuration. So think of SRS as a nine month activity, not five hours!

12. *Sensation, orgasm, libido.* I pity the poor girl who undergoes SRS mainly because of the erotic appeal, because she may wind up with none at all. Erotic responses vary all over the map, but you should be prepared for the possible worst case of being inorgasmic, having little vaginal sensation, and completely losing your sex drive. Even if you are lucky enough to have a fantastically erotic vagina, earth-shaking orgasms, and the sex drive of a tigress, you've still got a problem: nobody wants to date you, as we shall discuss in the next chapter.

13. *Long-term health care.* Don't forget that you now have a mix of male and female anatomy. You need to pay attention to the health care needs of both. You are still at risk of prostate cancer, at least until the hormones have caused it to shrink to a negligible size. I personally know of one trans woman who needed prostate surgery some years after her SRS. So make sure you are screened for it, until your doctor feels it is no longer necessary. Self-exams and mammograms for breast cancer are

recommended, even though I haven't heard of any cases of trans women contracting breast cancer. You don't have a cervix, but some gynecologists nevertheless recommend pap smears, even though they are primarily intended to detect cervical cancer.

14. *Profound feelings.* Most people seem to discover unexpected and profound feelings erupting after SRS. One girl described a feeling of cloudiness: "I just don't seem able to focus and get projects done with the same (admitted) obsession with time and deadlines that I had previously. My mind wanders into aimless reveries when I try to read, particularly if the reading material is technical and boring." Another girl had this reaction: "I feel like I've fallen apart completely. I need to make some radical changes in my life. None of the old ways work for me anymore. It's an awful experience." A wise long-time post-op explained it this way: "I suppose it's like the reaction after a sporting event, college exams or with any other event that you prepared and worked so hard toward. Give yourself a little time to 'download' and it will come back to you as it did with me and with most others I have talked with." Even with my cynical streak, I have to admit that SRS has affected me more profoundly than my nose job or other changes. I never accepted the idea that SRS was necessary to "complete me as a woman"; but now I feel that at least I've completed my body-modification project. In fact, I don't think I'm going to bother with breast implants, despite my tiny AA's. I'm done. I feel like I'm now on top of the heap of the

transgender hierarchy, despite my best efforts to respect all our paths as equals. (Part of that feeling comes from the new deference that cross-dressers and pre-ops seem to give me.) I have trouble understanding how a girl can consider herself to be transsexual, but not be doing her damnedest to get her SRS — even though intellectually I grant the legitimacy of other choices. I find myself thinking and saying, "I'm not transgender, I'm post-transsexual", in spite of my belief in inclusiveness. I find myself drifting away from my former friends, even as I resolve not to be one of "those" post-ops. I feel a greater right to take my place in women's spaces. I feel a relief that I'm not hiding anything any more, especially not that particularly masculine little thingie. Sex partners (okay, there have been a few) seem to treat me with more respect, more like I'm a delicate little flower. People ask me what it feels like to have a vagina; it doesn't feel like anything, it just feels right. Having a penis felt wrong. I'm very happy I had my SRS.

When the deed is done

When all is said and done, gals, you wind up with a vagina. Big woop. Let me tell you, a vagina is a lot more trouble than a penis. Besides dilating, you'll probably get yeast infections and maybe urinary infections; you'll need pads and tampons; and you need to sit when you pee. (But you are already doing that, aren't you?) You may find that a vagina is like a boat or a pool: You're better off with a friend who lets you use their's, than to have all the upkeep and maintenance of owning your own.

In spite of all that, I have to tell you, I like my vagina.

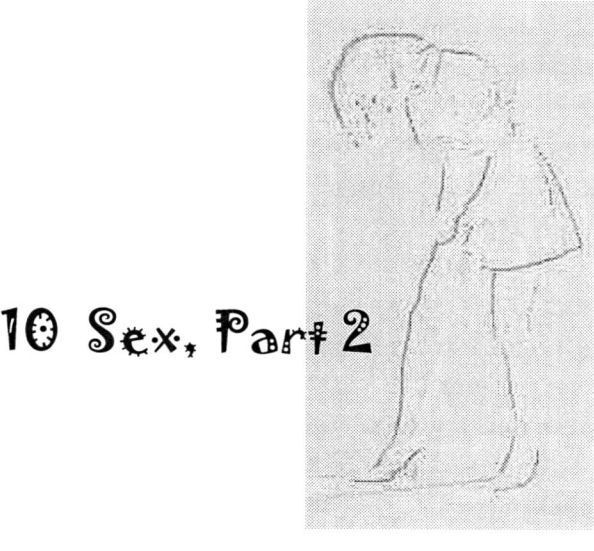

10 Sex, Part 2

*I*s there sex after SRS? Yes and no. For some people, yes.

For others, opportunities to use their new equipment for its most pleasurable purpose may occur rarely, if ever.

If you explored various modes of sexuality during your transition, maybe you found some particular thing or things you like. If so, fine; by all means, continue to pursue those avenues of delight. But chances are, if you are like most trans people, you've discovered that your favorite thing is just plain old vanilla sex with someone you care about deeply.

As a post-transsexual, that is, one who has had their gender dysphoria cured (whether or not you had surgery), your challenge now is to find a partner who will love you as a whole person, not just a sexual fetish. This is a difficult task for any person, and your special background makes it even harder.

When I began living as a woman, one of the many things that took me by surprise was the discovery that women do not get "hit on"—propositioned for sex or asked out on dates—all the time. (Having had little dating experience, I was also naïve about realizing that dating, for adults, is pretty much synonymous with having sex.) I had always had the common male perception that any woman could have sex any time she wanted with any man she chose. I thought that men constantly made passes at women in grocery stores, on the street, at church—any time and everywhere. Not so—unless you happen to be young, petite, and blonde. For the rest of us, propositions and invitations for dates are a rare and valued thing. Men are a lot shyer and more afraid of rejection than I realized. (I thought that was just me.) If guys only knew how far they could get by giving me, or any other woman, just a little bit of respectful attention and a few compliments, there would be a lot more actual sex going on in this world!

Disclosure

If you are patient, sooner or later somebody will take an interest in you. Congratulations! The next thing that happens, unfortunately, is that you confront the question of when to tell your partner about your transsexuality. It seems unfair to have to tell at all. Isn't it a private matter between you and your doctor? Isn't it something that is entirely in your past? Fair or not, the fact of the matter is that everybody with whom you have an intimate relationship will consider this to be an important thing for them to know about you. It goes back to how fundamental gender is to a person's identity, as we discussed in Chapter 1. Most people, sadly, are simply not equipped to deal with an intimate partner who has changed sex. It's not that they're bigoted or small-minded; it's just something built in, like sexual orientation. There's no use trying to fight it or change it. Just accept it and move on.

Unless you are living in "deep stealth" mode, having totally expunged all traces of your other-gendered past from your life (see Chapter 11), you probably need to inform your lover of your special quality sooner or later. If you don't tell, then at some point there is bound to be something that "outs" you—be that a wrong comment from a knowing friend, or finding this very book on your nightstand! Better that he or she should hear it from your own lips.

You probably need to disclose to your lover sooner or later, and "later" is a risky choice. Informing a partner during or after sex may lead to violence. When a man learns that the woman he just had sex with "used to be a man" or "is really a man," as he thinks of it, he may lash out "to prove that he's not homosexual"—although how beating or killing the woman does this, I don't understand. Besides being a safety risk, in my opinion waiting until later also disrespects your partner's right to informed consent, which is a prime tenet of proper sexual conduct.

Many people follow the policy of telling after a few dates but before having sex. Most people don't (at least they shouldn't) drag out all their dirty laundry on the first date, so why should we drag out this particular smelly sock? It seems to make sense to let your date get to know you as a whole person before bringing up this one thing which is apt to dominate his thinking once he hears it. Besides, by the third date he will like you so much that he won't let this little thing get in the way of a beautiful relationship, right? (Unfortunately not right, as it usually turns out.) In any event, if the whole thing fizzles out before the moment of truth, as it so often does, then the whole disclosure thing can be avoided.

I have heard some stories in which the "telling after a few dates" strategy worked out perfectly. Sometimes the guy was shocked and it took him a little while to decide he was all right with it, but good relationships and even marriages ensued.

For a while I tried a policy of disclosing "soonest"—as soon I think something there is a chance that something might develop between us. When I would get asked out on a date I would say, "I'd love to, but did you know I've had a sex change?" (One time I told this to somebody and he, befuddled, replied, "Which way?") I figured that we might as well get it over with. If the guy ran, he ran. At least we wouldn't have wasted our time and emotional investment on something that could not work. The outcome of this approach was that the guys were always grateful for my openness and honesty…but I never went out on any dates!

When I decided to start dating without disclosing my past, my first pleasant surprise was to find out that I could get away with it! It was final confirmation that I was 100% passable, even in intimate one-on-one situations. My second surprise was that I found it to be a bit challenging to talk about myself without bringing up my transsexuality. I'm not talking about the lying part (another surprise was that I found it quite easy to talk about my ex-*husband* and when I was a little *girl;*) rather, it was that I had spent so much of my last few years focused on my gender issues and my transition, I had let the rest of my life and my personality atrophy. Dating was a good exercise to help me rebuild my identity as a whole person, leaving behind the "trans" part as just something I dealt with in the past, not something central to my present day-to-day life. To my amazement, I had achieved my goal of becoming a normal woman; now it was time for me to enjoy it!

Actually, it turns out that any woman, even a trans woman, can get laid any time she wants—if she can locate a swingers party or a sex club like San Francisco's Power Exchange. In this type of environment, disclosing my sex change seems to be less of an issue, because the guys there really aren't too picky about how they get what they came for. Of course, meaningless sex with strangers is no substitute for the real thing, but sometimes it can fulfill a need.

Trans life partners

A few happily married trans women have told me that, as far as their husbands are concerned, they never really were men; they were just women with birth defects. That's the kind of fellow I am looking for. I like that attitude, because that's how I think of myself, too.

In my experience, the fact that I am post-op makes little difference to most men. I may have just as well have told them, "I have a penis" as "I have had a sex change operation." It is just as big of a turnoff. (Except for guys who *like* girls with penises—but that's a different matter entirely.) To put it crudely, to the vast majority of guys, I am simply not fuckable—in a more profoundly fundamental way than is the most hideously ugly non-transsexual woman. Even beer goggles cannot fix this problem, which seems to stem from guys' deep-seated fears that they may be homosexual. (I have a theory that the propagation of the species demands that most people evolve not just preferring heterosexuality, but they must actually abhor homosexuality; because, who would bother with the hassle of relating to the other gender if you could be sexually satisfied within your own?)

It may be a little easier for trans people, women or men, to find female partners than male partners, because woman generally seem to have less of an aversion to homosexuality than do straight men. Men also tend to have a very narrow comfort zone when dealing with genitals—they will gleefully lick or screw the nastiest vagina, but they blanch when confronted with a nice, clean box of tampons.

Likewise, they are extremely distressed by the thought of what we trans people may have done with our genitals. Having dealt with vaginal maintenance all their lives, women can usually take in stride our special experiences.

I've seen estimates that one quarter of trans women wind up in relationships with other trans women. That's certainly one way to get around the problem of people who simply cannot understand our plight. Another way is a relationship between a trans woman and a trans man; this has worked great for a few lucky couples.

Sadly, many trans women and trans men never find accepting life partners. I suppose that is true of many non-trans women and men as well, yes?

Enough about relationships, what about sex?

This chapter is titled "Sex", so I guess I had better get down to it.

Your first concern, if you had SRS, may be whether or not you are capable of orgasm. Some girls are wonderfully surprised by an orgasm during dilation just a week or two after surgery. Most require more time—six months, a year, or even longer. The delay may be due in part to how long it takes for the insulted nerves to heal and to remap their new pathways in your brain. Another reason is simply how long it takes to get yourself back into the right frame of mind. For comparison, consider how long it takes women to be ready for sex again after giving birth, which is similarly traumatic to the groin region. I myself, nine months out of surgery as I write this, have experienced a few orgasms in my sleep (are they still called "wet dreams" for females?), but nothing in my waking moments. My clitoris and vagina are sensate, so I think the problem is mostly in my head at this point. I believe that all of the top SRS surgeons working today have a high success rate at creating a sensate clitoris and a vagina that are physically capable of achieving orgasm. Nevertheless, research suggests that perhaps half of all trans women never become regularly orgasmic after surgery.

When you are physically and emotionally ready for sex after your SRS, you will need to find a partner that is particularly patient and understanding. No matter how sexually active you may have been with your penis, you are vaginal virgin and you need to learn how to have sex all over again. It won't be the first time you have been poked down there, not by a long shot, because you will have spent large portions of many days dilating your vagina, as we discussed in the previous chapter. But having another person involved, using a penis instead of a stent, and having sexual pleasure as the objective, is a much different experience. You may have trouble finding the vaginal entrance. Be careful, if you don't want some surprise back-door action! You will be unusually tight—especially for a woman your age. You will probably need to use some artificial lubricant; you'll have plenty on hand from your dilating. Insist on using a latex condom to prevent STDs (sexually transmitted diseases), and make sure the lubricant is water-based, as oil-based lubes can damage condoms.

How deep is your love?

What about size? There seems to be a "magic number" floating around that says your SRS surgeon should strive to achieve a vaginal depth of six inches. Most trans women seem to claim that they have six inches of depth, if not seven or eight. If so, I have come up a bit short, as I only have about four inches. Dr. Anne Lawrence wrote a paper (*Notes on Genital Dimensions,* available on her Web site) that suggests that my results may be quite typical, and, in any case, should not be a problem. According to Lawrence, vaginas of women who were born with them range in depth from three to six inches, and erect male penises average about five to six inches. So the experience of the vagina being unable to accommodate the partner's entire penis is probably more common for non-trans than trans women and should not be an impediment to a good sex life.

Besides vaginal depth, there is also the dimension of width to be considered. I know my vaginal width with extreme accuracy because of the stents I have been using to dilate. I and many other trans women use the standard stent set from Duratek Plastics of Saskatchewan, Canada. It includes five stents with diameters ranging from one inch to one and one half inches, in one eighth inch increments. When I first began dilating, it seemed unbelievable to me that I would ever move beyond the first couple of stents. Each time I stepped up to a larger stent size, it hurt a lot for a few days. But now I dilate easily with the largest stent. I usually start with a smaller one to loosen up and to work on trying to increase my depth, and then I use the one and a half incher to maintain my width. (Some girls name their stents; the largest one might be "Big John" for example.) This should be sufficient to accommodate any penis I am likely to encounter and I plan to stop at this point. Some girls keep going, to as much as two inches in diameter.

Sexual feeling

Don't be surprised if the focus of your sexual feelings changes. For a man, sex is all about touching the woman, and then about getting his penis to climax. As a woman, I find that sex is all about me being touched—all over my body, not just my genitals. I finally understand about foreplay! In fact, when the guy's erection comes into play I feel that the best part is over for me, because now the focus changes to *that thing*. Perhaps I will come to enjoy the actual in-and-out part more, but I think this feeling is fairly typical for women.

Another thing that has changed for me, and I wish I could think of a more delicate way to put this, is that all the other things a guy can do for me besides just sex and companionship has become a lot more important to me. What kind of car he drives makes a difference. It's not exactly that I'm a gold digger. It's just that being taken care of, materially as well as emotionally, feels very good to me, so a guy's capacity to take care of all my needs means a lot. It's not that I won't date a poor guy—but if I guy has money to spend on me, I won't look so critically at his appearance!

Most pleasantly, I find that performance anxiety is wonderfully absent from sex now that I have a vagina instead of a penis. I never realized how much men are on the line for getting and maintaining erections. Of course, I never had any problems in that area myself! Seriously, I am amazed at how relaxed I am in bed now that the erection is not my responsibility. Oh, I am happy to do what I can to help out; but ultimately the erection is my partner's job. Good luck with that, and let me know when you're ready! (By the way, he needs to be good and ready—meaning hard—if he's going to penetrate my extra-tight vagina.)

The flip-side of performance anxiety, however, is freshness anxiety. While I no longer worry about what I need to do once I hit the sheets, I constantly worry about whether I am clean and fresh enough to avoid embarrassment if it comes to that. It's funny, actually, because I know how little guys care about that; but I know just how nasty my little garden can get, so I worry about keeping it nice down there.

If you, as a trans woman, are convinced that penetrative, vaginal sex is not important to you, you may consider having a modified SRS to remove your penis and testicles and create a visually pleasing vulva, including a sensate clitoris, but without an actual vaginal cavity. This is an easier surgery since the PC muscle does not need to be penetrated and a vaginal canal does not need to be constructed, eliminating concerns about scrotal electrolysis or skin grafts. Best of all, you escape the pain and hassle of dilating. Some surgeons will be glad to perform this type of surgery for you. It is better to have no vaginal cavity at all than to have one which you do not care for properly. If you have a vagina but you do not faithfully dilate it, it will shrink up; then your gynecologist will not be able to insert an ice-cold speculum to see inside, and you will have problems when you have yeast infections or anything else going wrong in there.

♥ ♥ ♥

11 Starting a new life

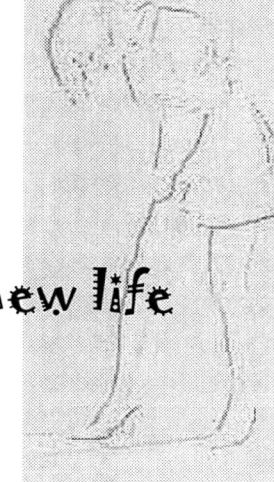

After we change sexes (with or without SRS, depending on our personal preferences), trans women and trans men often find that their goals and motivations in life change significantly. What used to be important doesn't matter any more, and feelings and relationships take on fresh new meaning. Many find a rebirth of spirituality in their lives. With the heavy yoke of gender confusion lifted, we are free to build new lives in harmony with our deep understanding of our true selves.

Every trans person finds that transition causes profound changes to the most important relationships in their lives.

Many marriages do not survive a spouse's gender transition. In those marriages that do survive, the couples need to work out new ways of relating to each other and new meanings for their relationships. Bonds with children and close family may be broken forever, or they may be capable of being rebuilt on new, firmer foundations; they may be strengthened by tempering in the forge of transition. Friendships that formed during transition may lose their meaning after transition is completed, and they may quickly fall by the wayside. Like someone who moves to a new city or a new country, the post-trans person must search out new friends and possibly new lovers with whom they can build new lives.

Many people change their jobs and even careers during or after their gender transition. All too often this decision is made for them, because their employer fires them as soon as they hear about it. But many people tenaciously hold on to their jobs through their transition, with generous support from their employers, only to discover after transition that they don't want to spend their lives doing that job any more. In my case, I built a successful career as a computer hardware engineer. When I got laid off just in time for my SRS, I happily decided I would never return to the high tech field. Frankly, I was bored to death and sick of the whole computer industry independently of my gender issues; but at that point I suddenly felt that I would prefer to spend my time helping people instead of focusing so much on inanimate things. I returned to school and now I'm studying to be a nurse. (Update: I gave up that goal and now I'm studying technical writing. See how things change?)

Post-transition is also a great opportunity to find new hobbies and activities, and perhaps revive or retire some old ones. For example, I traded nightclub dancing for ballroom dancing. And I was delighted to realize that I could attend Stanford Bachelors Club singles mixers, now as one of the cute chicks who all the guys are after! (All the guys aren't after me, as it turned out, but I still have a lot of fun.)

Stealth

Like the B-2 stealth bomber that flies virtually invisible to the enemy's radar, many people choose to keep their transsexual past invisible to all around them. We call this living in stealth mode, or "woodworking"—blending into the woodwork. Nobody agrees on an exact definition of stealth, and variant terms abound. For someone living in "deep stealth," nobody in her current life knows about her true past, and all clues about her sex change have been carefully hidden and expunged. Even her spouse or significant other may not know. Deep stealth means living with a certain amount of tension because you have to be constantly vigilant to protect your secret; you are never free from the fear that something might "out" you. But the reward is great: to be able to live an absolutely "normal" life at last.

Many trans people live in a more relaxed stealth mode, sharing their past with close friends and loved ones, but not with coworkers or other social friends and acquaintances, and subtly concealing it whenever possible. Some descriptive terms for this strategy include situational, compartmentalized, selective, or functional stealth.

Others, like me, are casually "out" whenever it comes up, especially when it may be useful to crusade for the rights of transsexual and transgender people. A few wear their transsexuality on their sleeves, or literally on their "Transsexual Menace" tee shirts.

I think it is natural to be less stealthy immediately after transition, while the issue looms so large in our minds. Indeed, most of us go through a phase where we are not very passable, so we are forced to learn to be "out and proud" from necessity. It is difficult to unlearn this attitude and change to one of stealth, if we so choose. Those who abruptly go "deep stealth," moving to a new city and abandoning all contact with people who knew them from before, must find it hard at first to keep from outing themselves. As the months and years go by, transition and our former transsexualism and gender dysphoria fade from our minds and our day-to-day experience. We fall into a stealthy existence because why in the world would the subject ever come up? Our new friends and acquaintances never know about our past, and those who knew us before forget about it since we blend so naturally into our new roles. If we occasionally disclose our past to a friend, she only looks puzzled and asks herself, "Why is she telling me this? What does she expect me to do with that information?" Besides, dealing with trans issues day in and day out gets tiring; the urge to simply leave it all behind and live in stealth is alluring. (It may be similar for a spouse who is initially supportive, but who eventually gets tired of it all and decides to ask for a divorce.) My own strategy is not to worry about how stealthy I live, and just let it develop on its own.

Trans marriage

Suppose I do find a fellow who wants to marry me and whom I want to marry. Don't laugh; it could happen! Can we legally get married? Generally speaking, no, we cannot. Under the law in all fifty United States, I am still legally my birth gender as far as getting married is concerned. On the other hand, I look like a woman and my driver's license, passport, and birth certificate say I'm female. There is nothing to prevent me from marrying as a woman. Many trans people go ahead and do this, and appear to have all the trappings of legal marriage.

The problem arises if someone challenges the validity of the marriage in a court of law, as might happen in disputes over divorce, inheritance, insurance claims, etc. For example, two key cases in current case law are Littleton and Gardiner. In 1999 in the great state of Texas, trans woman Christie Lee Littleton was prevented from filing a lawsuit over the wrongful death of her husband because the marriage was ruled to be invalid. The court reasoned that gender is determined from chromosomes, not genitals; furthermore Christie Lee's chromosomes were simply assumed to be XY because her birth certificate originally said "Male", and so Christie Lee Littleton was a man as far as the court was concerned. Meanwhile, in Kansas, Joe

Gardiner was challenging the inheritance of his father's $2.5 million fortune by his foster mother, J'Noel Gardiner, a trans woman. First the decision went to Joe; then in 2001 an appeals court threw it back into play, rejecting the Littleton reasoning. But finally, in 2002 the Kansas Supreme Court determined that J'Noel's marriage was same-sex and therefore invalid, and Joe got the dough. The bottom line is that legality of trans people's marriage is ambiguous, but court judgments have been running against us.

On the other hand, a sex change never affects the validity of an existing marriage. If your dear wife stays with you after your sex change, you can be a happy, perfectly legal lesbian couple. At least, in the in the U.S., that is. In Great Britain there are cases where couples have been told they must divorce prior to sex reassignment surgery.

The best solution to this mess would be for courts to grant changes of gender to transsexuals the same way they grant name changes; that is, such that the new gender designation would be binding for all legal purposes including marriage. Some legal challenges are being raised to attempt to further this aim, there is no political muscle behind it and it doesn't seem likely to be achieved in the foreseeable future. In the meanwhile, the legalization of same-sex marriage seems likely to come about shortly, and it will render moot the trans marriage dilemma. Legalization of same-sex marriage removes gender requirements from the marriage contract. Once marriage is defined as a union between two *persons,* the question of whether one or both of those persons may have had a sex change will be irrelevant from a legal standpoint.

Some transsexual people view the same-sex marriage issue as something that doesn't concern them because they are not gay; they feel that validating their marriages under such laws would deny their true gender status. If same-sex relationships are relegated to civil unions or some other contract besides marriage, this would be true. We would be forced to determine which type of contract we would be allowed to enter into in our own particular relationships. But if marriage is simply marriage for all couples, it seems to me that solves all of our issues as trans people and we should enthusiastically support it. Conversely, if the Federal Marriage Amendment (a proposed amendment to the Constitution of the Unites States of America that would permanently deny marriage rights to same-sex couples) passes, trans marriages will be thrown into legal disarray. Likewise, I believe it is important to overturn DOMA, the federal Defense Of Marriage Act signed by President Clinton in 1996. For purposes of federal benefits, DOMA defines " marriage" as a union between a man and a woman, and then allows states to refuse to recognize same-sex marriages performed in other states.

I hope that by the time you read this, same-sex marriage has become generally accepted in all the states (and all the world, for that matter), and you cannot understand why I am making such a big fuss about it!

Growing old trans

When I first began to consider that I might change my sex, I worried, *Being a pretty young woman would be lots of fun, but what would it be like to be a woman at 70, 80, or 90 years old?* Later I came to realize that what I would really hate is to be an 80 year old *man!* In fact, the idea of being a frail little old lady is rather appealing to me now, which is a good thing, since it won't be very long before it becomes a reality!

A sex change may add additional load to the burdens of old age. However, with foresight, a good support system, and a little bit of luck, your problems should be minimal. Here are some issues to consider as you plan for your trans old age.

1. Physically the surgeries and hormones shouldn't be a problem; just don't go overboard with too many face lifts or you'll wind up like Joan Rivers.

2. If you're estranged from your family, they won't be there to support you when you're old. Try to build a new "family" of friends that you can depend when you need them.

3. Medical care may be refused at some facilities. The movie *Southern Comfort* documented the struggles of trans man Robert Eads, a frequent speaker at the Southern Comfort transgender conferences, who died of cervical and ovarian cancer after 20 doctors refused to treat him

because he was trans. So be sure to line up good medical care that you can rely on in your old age.

4. On a similar note, you may be refused entry in retirement homes or nursing homes because of your sex change. Gender presentation and gender expression are not protected classes in most states and municipalities, like race, creed, and color are, so it is perfectly legal for managed care facilities (and employers) to discriminate against trans people. So again, it may be more difficult to find the care you need in your old age. Meanwhile, while you are young, please work to get laws passed to make discrimination based on gender presentation and gender expression illegal everywhere. (Courts in the European Community are making great strides in this area; they are moving much more quickly than anywhere in the U.S.)

5. Private medical insurance is difficult and expensive to obtain these days in any case. You can bet that any evidence of your sex change in your medical records will be used as a reason to deny your application. So be very careful about planning for your medical insurance needs. For example, if you are on a plan that is working for you, you may want to stay with it even if the costs seem unreasonably high. Or, you may want to pay closer attention to insurance benefits, on the job and in retirement, when you choose an employer.

6. In the previous section we talked about how your marriage may be open to legal challenge if you've had a

sex change. Until laws become firmer in this area, it is a good idea to set up separate contracts to designate power of attorney and who can make decisions about your medical care and visit you in the hospital. Make a will. (There was no will in the J'Noel Gardiner case—and with a $2.5 million estate, can you imagine?) A living will, which specifies your wishes about when to pull your plug —that is, whether you wish to be kept alive on artificial life support, and a durable medical power of attorney should be in place in case you become disabled. Don't forget to specify any funeral arrangements that are important to you—I don't want my old boy name on my tombstone!

On the bright side, changing your sex seems to automatically take off about ten years, so you will probably age more gracefully than others of your new gender. Also, any problems you might have in passing are likely to diminish, since old men and old women look more and more alike.

The popularity of sex reassignment surgery began growing in the 1970's and 1980's, so we are just now starting to develop a significant population of geriatric transsexual women and men. The trans community is starting to pay attention to the special problems of our aging members and beginning to develop some support resources for them. This issue alone is a good reason to continue to support a vital community among transsexuals, in camaraderie with other transgender peoples, rather than all of us spinning off into isolated stealth lives.

A happy and productive future

Like changing your sex, building a happy and productive future may be difficult to accomplish, but the process is simple. It will be fully explained in my next book, *How To Have A Life: A Lighthearted Look At Building A Happy And Productive Future For You And Your Loved Ones.* I plan to start writing it as soon as I figure it out myself.

A Lighthearted* Glossary of Terms

*★ *Lighthearted is* my disclaimer; people in the "gender community" (see below) will argue about anything, and most especially about definitions of terms!

Androgyne

A person who lives without obvious gender markers; may consider his/herself to be both man and woman, or neither, or something completely different.

Autogynephilia

A word that is guaranteed to raise a ruckus in any group of transsexual people.

Blow Job

Oral sex involving a penis; also known as a *hummer;* (important note: you don't actually blow on it; but you might want to hum on it).

BDSM

Bondage Discipline Dominance Submission Sadism Masochism; a broad category of kinky sex practices usually involving tying and flogging or spanking.

BLT

Bacon, lettuce, and tomato sandwich (not to be confused with GLBT).

Clock (verb)

To identify someone as something other than what that as which they present themselves; a cross-dresser is clocked when someone sees them and says, "That woman is a man!"; same as read.

Cross-dresser

A man who dresses in women's clothes for sexual pleasure or just because he finds it relaxing; usually identifies as a male (unless he is on his way to transsexualism).

CD

Cross-dresser.

Cinderella complex

When an adult thinks of herself [himself] as a fairy tale princess.

Dilate, Dilation

The process of inserting a stent into the neovagina to prevent it from shrinking and to train the pubococcygeus (PC) muscle to relax.

Dildo

An artificial penis usually used for sex play. If it runs on electricity and vibrates, it's a vibrator.

DQ

Drag Queen.

Drag Queen

A male, usually gay, cross-dressed in an exaggerated feminine presentation; often an entertainer (as in dr*ag* perform*er or drag show)*.

Drag King

The female equivalent of a drag queen; a female, usually lesbian, cross-dressed in an exaggerated masculine presentation; often an entertainer.

Ex-transsexual

A person who has completed a gender transition and who no longer suffers from gender dysphoria; also post-transsexual.

Faux Drag Queen

A female that looks like a drag queen.

Female Impersonator

A male who entertains by imitating female characters or celebrities.

FTM, F2M

A female to male transsexual person.

GD

Gender dysphoria; mental pain and confusion arising from an uncertain gender identity or a gender identity that does not match with the body's anatomical sex.

Gender

Whether a person is a woman or a man (by the binary model); or where a person is on a continuum which stretches from completely woman to partially woman and partially man, to completely man (by the continuum model); or maybe something completely different by other models; in any case, it is more directly related to *gender identity* than to sex.

Gender Binary

The idea that every person is either a man or a woman, and no other possibilities exist.

Gender Community

Some say there is no such thing as a gender community; we're all separate groups. Others think that transgender, transsexual, and intersex people, along with drag queens, cross-dressers, gender queers, she-males, and anybody else who doesn't fit nicely into the gender binary need to act as a community to work for our rights, which are simply human rights.

Gender Identity

The internal sense that a person is a woman or a man, or possibly a combination of the two, or even something else entirely.

Gender Presentation, Gender Expression

The signals a person gives by his or her dress, makeup, demeanor, speech, etc. which act as cues that he or she wishes to be accepted and treated as a particular gender, that is, as a woman or as a man.

Genderqueer

A person who lives with mixed gender markers; may consider his/herself to be both man and woman, or neither, or something completely different; also known as *genderfuck* because they sometimes like to fuck with peoples' heads.

GID

Gender identity disorder; the condition that afflicts *transsexual* people.

GLBT

Gay, lesbian, bisexual, transgender.

Google (verb)

To use the www.google.com search engine to find information on the Internet.

GRS

Genital reconstruction surgery or genital repurposing surgery; same as SRS.

Harry Benjamin Standards of Care

HBIGDA's guidelines for the medical care of people afflicted with transsexualism.

HBIGDA

The Harry Benjamin International Gender Dysphoria Association, Inc.

Hermaphrodite

A person born with sexually ambiguous genitalia.

Hormones

Chemical substances which act as messengers to activate and regulate processes in the body; in the gender community, it usually refers to the sex hormones, estrogen for females and testosterone for males.

HRT

Hormone replacement therapy, as for menopausal women.

Hummer

Same as *blow job*.

Intersex

A person with an intersex condition is born with sex chromosomes, external genitalia, or an internal reproductive system that is not considered "standard" for either male or female.

Labels

Terms like *transsexual* and *cross-dresser* which indicate simplistic descriptions or categorizations of people. Labels are good because they allow us to communicate a great deal of information about ourselves and others in a very efficient way. Labels are evil because they deny our individuality and lead us and others to make mistaken assumptions about what we truly are.

LGBT

Same as *GLBT*, except ladies first.

LGBTTIQQ

Lesbian, gay, bisexual, transgender, transsexual, intersex, questioning, queer.

Man

Related to gender; term is too difficult to define rigorously.

MTF, M2F

A male to female transsexual person.

Neovagina

A new vagina created by SRS.

Non

Sometimes used as shorthand for *non-transgender person* to avoid the inaccurate use of the term *normal*.

Non-op

Non-operative transsexual person, one who does not plan to ever have sex reassignment surgery.

Normal

What most of us want to be, but nobody really is.

Orchiectomy

Surgery to remove the male testes (if you are a cow we would call it *castration*); usually done as part of sex reassignment surgery; pre-op and non-op transsexuals may have just an orchiectomy to eliminate testosterone production and hence allow them to reduce their hormone intake; orchiectomy is also used to treat advanced prostate cancer, which thrives on testosterone.

Penis

The male sex organ (the outie kind); most men are fortunate enough to be born with one.

Post-op

A post-operative transsexual person; one who has undergone sex reassignment surgery; now an ex-transsexual person.

Post-transsexual

A person who has completed a gender transition and who no longer suffers from gender dysphoria; also *ex-transsexual*.

Pre-op

Pre-operative transsexual person, one who has not had sex reassignment surgery yet.

Read

Same as *clock*; getting *read* and getting *clocked* both mean than someone spotted that you are transgender or transsexual.

Sex

Among other things, this refers to whether a person has genitals conforming to the common male configuration or the common female configuration.

She-male

A person with female sex characteristics including breasts but whose genitals are male; usually identifies as male; often a sex worker or pornography performer.

Significant Other (S.O.)

The lover with whom you share your life, but to whom you may not be legally married.

SOC

In the gender community, this usually refers to the Harry Benjamin Standards Of Care.

SRS

Sex reassignment surgery; plastic surgery which changes a penis to a vagina or vice-versa (vice-versa is a lot more difficult).

Stent

A plastic rod used for *dilating* the *vagina;* similar to a dildo.

T-boy

A transgender or transsexual man.

Glossary

T-girl

A transgender or transsexual woman.

Trannie

Short for *transsexual* or *transvestite*.

Trannie Admirer

A man who is attracted to t-girls; usually means that they like to give blow jobs to t-girls (that's right, *give to*, not *get from*).

Trannie Chaser

Same as *trannie admirer*.

Trannie-friendly Lighting

Dim lighting as in a restaurant or nightclub, in which is a *t-girl* is less likely to be *clocked*.

Tranny

Variation of *trannie;* (*trannie* is the preferred spelling, because it matches with Lannie, as in *Lannie the Trannie*!)

Transgender

1. A person whose gender identity does not fit neatly into the male/female binary model.
2. A person who is confused about their gender identity;
3. an umbrella term that includes anyone (e.g., transsexuals as well as transgenders) who doesn't fit into traditional male/female gender stereotypes.

Transition

1. The process of changing one's gender presentation for the one s/he was born and raised with to one which matches his/her internal

gender identity.
2. The act of beginning to live full time in a new gender identity; as in, *Lannie Rose transitioned on January 1, 2002.*

Trans Man

A transsexual man or an ex-transsexual man (a *trans man* was born with a vagina).

Transsexual

A condition wherein a person has genitals corresponding to one gender but an inner gender identity corresponding to another; this condition may be cured by *triadic therapy*.

Transvestite

Another term for *cross-dresser*; generally considered somewhat pejorative today.

Trans Woman

A transsexual woman or an ex-transsexual woman (a *trans woman* was born with a penis).

Triadic Therapy

The three-step process recommended in the Harry Benjamin Standards Of Care for treating transsexualism; the three steps are: living in the preferred gender presentation; hormones; and SRS.

TS

A transsexual person.

Tuck, Tucking

Most t-girls *tuck* their penises back between their legs to keep smooth lines in tight outfits (for a good *tuck*, the testicles are pushed up into the abdominal cavity, not pulled back with the penis); some cross-dressers don't bother to tuck and some trannie chasers are actually turned on by a noticeable bulge in a skirt.

Two Trannie Rule

principle that the likelihood of getting *clocked* increases exponentially with the number of transgender people seen together; e.g., two trannies are four times as likely to be clocked as a single trannie alone; three trannies are nine times as likely to be clocked, etc.

Vagina

The female sex organ (the innie kind); most women are fortunate enough to be born with one.

Vampire

Like Dracula, a creature (in our case, a *t-girl*) that comes out only at night and must never be seen in daylight; usually found in nightclubs and bars that cater to gays and trannies (and most especially in bars with *trannie-friendly lighting.*)

Vibrator

An artificial penis that runs on electricity and vibrates, usually used for sex play.

Weenie Roast

A party thrown for a trans woman just before her SRS; hot dogs are served in honor of the departing weenie.

Woman

Related to gender; term is too difficult to define rigorously.

Further reading

This book has presented a fairly high level description of the sex change process. More detailed information is available in many great books and web sites. On the following pages are some of the ones that I found most useful. I've tried to list only resources that seem to have good staying power; my apologies in advance if any of these books have gone out of print or links have gone 404.

Books cited in the text

Anders, Charles, *The Lazy Crossdresser*, Greenery Press, 2002. A humorous and very practical guide to cross-dressing.

Brown, Mildred and Chloe Rounsley, *True Selves: Understanding Transsexualism - For Families, Friends, Coworkers, and Helping Professionals*, Jossey-Bass, 1996. Millie Brown, a well-known and well-loved gender therapist, presents a very readable and accurate description of the psychology and lives of transsexuals in this popular book.

Web sites cited in the text

www.tsroadmap.com, *TS Roadmap*; Andrea James's valuable site with detailed information about gender transition for transsexuals.

www.annelawrence.com/twr, *Transsexual Women's Resources*; Dr. Anne Lawrence's helpful site with medical and other information for transsexual women.

www.transparentcy.org, *Trans Parentcy;* supporting the loving and caring relationship between Transgender Parents and their children.

www.isna.org, *Intersex Society of North America;* all about intersex.

www.femimage.com, *FemImage;* Denaë Doyle's site for her unique service coaching trans women on feminine poise and deportment.

www.tgforum.com, *Transgender Forum;* e-zine for the transgender community, new content weekly; subscription service plus some free content.

http://store.yahoo.com/transgender/devfemvoic1.html, *Melanie Anne Phillips;* where to obtain *Develop A Female Voice* video or audio tape (or disk).

www.deepstealth.com/store, *Deep Stealth Products;* where to obtain Andrea James's *Finding Your Female Voice* (yes, that is the same Andrea James who runs TS Roadmap) and other trans-oriented products.

www.payless.com, *Payless ShoeSource;* shopping site for shoes.

www.onehanesplace.com, *One Hanes Place;* shopping site for nylons, brassieres, etc.

www.carabella.com, *Carabella Collection;* shopping site for sexy dresses.

www.threewisheslingerie.com, *Three Wishes Lingerie;* shopping site for lingerie.

www.ladybwear.com, *Lady Bwear;* shopping site for fetish wear.

www.realdoll.com, *Realdoll;* shopping site for amazing sex dolls.

www.google.com, *Google;* search engine.

Further Reading

More great books

Addams, Calpernia Sarah, *Mark 947: A Life Shaped by God, Gender and Force of Will,* Writers Club Press, 2002. Story of trans woman whose tragic relationship with a murdered soldier was depicted in the Showtime movie *Soldier's Girl.*

Boylan, Jennifer Finney, *She's Not There: A Life in Two Genders,* Broadway, 2003. Lighthearted memoir of a Colby College English professor who transitions from male to female.

Kirk, Sheila, M.D. & Martine Rothblatt, J.D., *Medical, Legal and Workplace Issues for the Transsexual,* Together Lifeworks, 1995. Excellent reference for legal and medical issues. [May be out of print.]

McCloskey, Deirdre, *Crossing: A Memoir*, Candlewick Press, 2001. Engrossing story of Nobel prize winning economist's harrowing life and transition from male to female.

Rose, Donna, *Wrapped in Blue: A Journey of Discovery,* Living Legacy Press, 2003. Memoir of software engineer's transition, very detailed about transition process and its effect on a very angry spouse and troubled son. (Note: Donna Rose is not related to this book's author.)

Stringer, Joanne Altman, *The Transsexual's Survival Guide II: To Transition & Beyond for Family, Friends, and Employers,* Creative Design Services, 1992. Good guide to coming out issues.

Stuart, Kim Elizabeth, *The Uninvited Dilemma: A Question of Gender,* Metamorphous Press, 1991. Excellent overview of transsexualism, a little less recent and more technical than True Selves.

Walworth, Janis, *Transsexual Workers: An Employer's Guide,* Center for Gender Sanity, 1998. A short an practical guide to transsexualism with an emphasis on workplace issues, an excellent resource for those transitioning on the job and their managers and HR people.

More great web sites

http://ai.eecs.umich.edu/people/conway/conway.html, *Dr. Lynn Conway;* very rich site full of infromation about all aspects of transsexuality and transition; see especially her pages showing successful trans women and men.

www.avitale.com, *Anne Vitale Ph.D.;* Anne is a licensed psychologist specializing in cross-dressing and gender identity ; her site has a lot of good psychology articles.

www.genderhappy.com, *Gender Happy;* dedicated to the concept that a tg can be happy and successful in life.

http://www.hbigda.org, *The Harry Benjamin International Gender Dysphoria Association, Inc. (HBIGDA);* a professional organization devoted to the understanding and treatment of gender identity disorders; *The HBIGDA Standards of Care for Gender Identity Disorders* are available on this site.

www.ntac.org, *NTAC, The National Transgender Advocacy Coalition;* a political action group.

www.transgenderlegal.com, *Transgender Legal, trans legal resources;* Phyllis Randolph Fry, the great trans woman lawyer and trans advocate, runs this site; sign up for her e-mail newletter, *The Phyllabuster.*

http://www.drschrang.com, *Dr. Eugene Schrang;* one of the most prominent SRS surgeons' Web site, complete with graphic photographs of his results.

http://www.intelleng.com/zen.html, *Zen and the Art of Post-Operative Maintenance;* care instructions for right after SRS surgery.

http://venusenvy.keenspace.com, *Venus Envy;* Erin Lindsey's wonderful online comic about a high-school age trans girl; Jade Gordon's *Lean On Me* at http://jadaze.keenspace.com has a similar theme.

Index

A

acrylics 121
activism 27
Adams apple 139
admirer 44
airport 28
anabolic steroids 98
anal sex 43, 136, 147, 163
Anders,Charles 10, 47
androgynous 11, 18pp., 82
anesthesia 144
anorexia 94
antiandrogen 98, 102
antibacterial soap 144
AsiaSF 23
Atlanta,Georgia 27
ATM cards 127

B

ballroom dancing 80, 167
balls,Ben Wa 46
balls,Duotone 46
banking 29, 126p., 136
Barbie doll 113
bargaining 58
bathroom 116, 129
battery-operated 119
BDSM 46pp.
beard 30, 96, 119
beauty parlor 114, 121p.
bedrooms,separate 60
bigotry 93, 155
bikini 81, 119, 132, 145
bisexual 25, 40, 42
blood 79, 98, 101
blow job 42pp.
bondage 25, 46p.
border-crossers 11
bottom 137, 140, 145, 170
boundaries 16, 40, 44, 48, 61
boutiques 31
bowl(toilet) 145p.
boy mode 90, 112, 121
brain 6pp., 89, 99, 112, 159
brassiere 30, 123
breast implants 123, 139pp., 149.
Brown,Mildred(Millie) 11
butch 19

C

caffeine 99
California 21p., 142
camera 47
Canada 138, 161

cancer   138, 148p., 172
Carabella   30
Carla   22p.
catheter   143, 145
celibacy   20, 41
certificate,birth   127, 169
cervix   149, 172
chaser,trannie   44p.
Cholon,Dr.Annette   142
chromosomes   6, 20, 169
cigars,cigarettes   78, 84
Cinderella complex   35
Clinton,President Bill   42, 171
clitoris   43, 46, 136, 144, 160, 163
clitoroplasty   136
clocking   25, 27, 33pp., 119, 133
closet   16, 19pp., 26, 47, 57, 107
clowns   40, 51
colon   136
Colorado   27, 93
compartmentalize   168
condom   43, 160
Constitution of the United States   171
corrective surgery   146
cosmetics   17, 67, 78
Cotillion,TGSF   21, 25
couples   24, 68, 159, 166, 170p.
coworkers   3, 11, 109, 167
cross-gender   17
cross-living   11p.
cunnilingus   43
custody   59p., 106, 110

D

denial   35, 55pp., 64, 87
Denver,Colorado   27
deportment   27, 31
depression   58, 73p., 88, 103
Dermablend   119
Different For Girls(movie)   10
dilation   144, 146p., 150, 159pp., 163p.
dildo   45, 146
disclosure   154pp., 168
Dissociative Identity Disorder   90
diversity   26p., 29p., 73
divorce   58pp., 63, 66, 94p., 169p.
DMV   126
do-it-yourself   21, 25p., 29, 98
documents   2, 28, 124
DOMA (Defense Of Marriage Act)   171
dominance   46p.
donut pillow   144
Doubtfire,Mrs.(movie)   10
douching   147
Doyle,Denaë   31
drag   10, 16, 24, 33pp., 123, 125, 156
dungeon   46pp.
Duratek Plastics   161
dysphoria,gender   6, 19, 58, 60, 75, 88p., 95, 132, 154, 168

E

eggs,banking   136, 138

elective surgery   83, 138, 168
electrolysis   101, 117pp., 142, 163
employers   111p., 115, 126, 166, 173
endocrinologist   79, 98, 101p.
epilator   120
erection   42, 46, 137, 161pp.
Esprit conference   27
Estevez,Emilio   93
estrogen   98, 102
exhibitionist   50
eyelashes   123

F

facial feminization surgery(ffs)   136, 139p.
fantasies   8, 69
fashion   22, 30, 47, 84, 143
female impersonators   16
femimage.com   31
feminization   19, 113, 139
Fenton,Jamie Faye   28
festivals   26, 110
fetish   41, 49pp., 154
fetus   7
ffs(facial feminization surgery)   136, 139p.
fingernails   2, 121, 123
firefighter   9p., 12
fistula   142
follicles   117p., 142
Folsom Street Fair   25
foreplay   162
furries   50

G

galvanic electrolysis   118
Gardiner,J'Noel   169p., 174
Gardiner,Joe   169p.
gender-ambiguous   124
gender-enhanced   16, 29
genetics   9, 44, 54, 136, 146
genital reconstruction surgery (GRS)   130
genitalian   129
Georgia   27
GG(genetic girl)   44p.
GID(gender identity disorder)   6, 89
Goodwill thrift store   17, 124
google   29p., 51
graft,skin   136, 142, 163
Green,Jamison   39
GRS(genital reconstruction surgery)   130
gynecologist   137, 149, 164

H

Halloween   35, 49
Harry Benjamin International Gender Dysphoria Association, Inc.   89
Harry Benjamin Standards of Care   99, 132
HBIGDA(Harry Benjamin International Gender Dysphoria Association)   89
HBO   10, 60
Hedwig   137

hemorrhage   142
herbal hormone precursors   98
hermaphrodite   6
heterosexual   24, 40p., 158
Hidden Woman,The   22
hobbies   4, 167
Hollywood   30
homosexuality   155, 158
HRT   102

I

identification   2, 28, 112, 124
incontinence   145
infection   142, 147, 150, 164
initials   124
injection   98, 140p.
innie   129
insulin   141
insurance   28, 126, 138, 144, 169, 173
Internet   11, 17, 29p., 51, 75, 93, 98, 107
intersex   6, 20
intimacy   65
Italian   129

J

jail   28p.
James,Andrea   31, 122
Japan   57
jaw reduction surgery   139
Jennifer(name)   124p.
Just Like A Woman(movie)   10

K

kissing   42
knives   47
knot   47
Kubler-Ross,Elisabeth   56

L

labia   137, 143, 147
labiaplasty   137, 144, 148
ladybwear.com   31
Lannie Rose   24, 105, 124
laser hair removal   118pp.
Lawrence,Dr.Anne   31, 161
Lazy Crossdresser,The   10, 47
letters,approval   28p., 127, 134, 139
LGBT(lesbian gay bisexual transgender)   25p.
libido   51, 101, 148
license,driver's   28, 125p., 169
lifestyle   41, 79
lingerie   6, 15, 31
liposuction   2, 141
Littleton,Christie Lee   169p.
lye   118

M

mail-order   17, 30
makeover   22
makeup   22, 30, 37, 80, 119
mall   25, 34, 80
mammogram   148

Martinez Jr.,Fred   93
masochism   46
mastectomy   137
maxi-pads   144p.
MCC(Metropolitan Community Church)   26
menopause   98, 102p.
merge,dressing style   25p., 56
Mexico   141
Michael(name)   124
Michelle(name)   124p.
mid-life crisis   56, 120
minoxidil   139
Mitchell,Pauline   93
Monistat   144
monograms   124
morality   15p., 41
morphine   143
mortgage   126
Mrs.Doubtfire(movie)   10
MTF(male to female transsexual)   3, 54, 80p., 98, 100pp., 136p.

N

nails(fingernails)   2, 114, 121, 123
naracotics   40
Navajo   93
Nebraska   28
neovagina   142, 146
Nevada   22
Newmar,Julie   10
nipples   114
non-operative transsexual   130
Normal(movie)   10, 60
nose job   87, 138p., 148p.

O

oil-based lubricant   160
Omaha,Nebraska   28
one-step SRS procedure   143p.
onehanesplace.com   30
Oprah Winfrey   95
oral sex   41pp., 144
orchiectomy   102, 136
orgasm   148, 159p.
orientation,sexual   39, 155
OSHA   115
outie   129
ovarian cancer   172

P

pap smear   149
parlor,beauty   114, 121p.
passing   5, 34, 36p., 121, 139, 174
passport   29, 127, 131, 169
patches,hormone   98, 103
Pauline Mitchell   93
Payless ShoeSource   30
pedicure   114
peeing   135, 143pp., 150
penectomy   136, 143
penetration   42, 44, 163
Phillips,Melanie Anne   122
pierced ears   114, 120
piercings   2, 114, 120
Pilates   81
pill,hormone   98p., 101
pillow,donut   144
PlanetOut   39
poise   31

post-op, post-operative   147, 149p., 158
post-transition   166
post-transsexual   150, 154
pre-op, pre-operative   129, 150
precursors, hormone   98
preference, sexual   8, 40, 165
pregnancy   40
President Clinton   171
press-on fingernails   121
Priscilla, Queen of the Desert (movie)   10
pronouns   18, 54
prostate   148
prosthetic penises   30
Prozac   58
psychiatrist   29, 134
psychologist   3, 92
PTA   112
pubococcygeus (PC) muscle   146

Q

queen, drag   10, 16, 24, 33p., 125
queer   95
quitting   83

R

razor   119
Realdoll   46
receding hairline   16, 139
registration, automobile   126
registration, voter   126
regret   132, 134, 138
Reid, Dr. Russell   29, 99
remora, removing the   129
Reno, Nevada   22
restroom   37p., 81, 114pp., 146
retirement   173
rhinoplasty   2, 130, 139
Rivers, Joan   91, 172
RLE (real life experience)   10, 47, 132pp., 139
Roadmap, TS   31
Rogaine   123, 139
Rose, Lannie   24, 105, 124
Ross (store)   17, 56
Rounsley, Chloe   11

S

same-sex marriage   170p.
San Jose, California   22
Santa Cruz, California   21, 26
Saskatchewan, Canada   161
scalp advance surgery   139
SCC (Southern Comfort Conference)   27
schizophrenia   88
Schrang, Dr. Eugene   137
SCOUT (Santa Cruz Organization Uniting Trans men)   21
scrotum   136p., 142, 163
Seattle, Washington   27
seepage   145
Seiko Cleancut Shaver   119
shaving   119p., 139
siblings   109
silicone   46, 123, 140p.
sister   9, 17, 27, 31, 100
skin graft   136, 142, 163

Southern Comfort Conference (SCC) 27p., 93, 172
speculum 164
sperm 136
sphincter 43, 145
spirituality 165
spironolactone 98
sports 54, 81, 114
standards of care(SOC) 99, 132, 134
Stanford Bachelors Club 167
Starbucks 99
stealth 122, 155, 167pp., 175
stent 56, 82, 89, 117, 141, 146p., 160pp.
stereotypes 70
steroids 98
Stud bar in San Francisco 24
suicide 62, 132
swingers parties 157

T

t-boy 45
Taiwan 95
tampons 147, 150, 158
tattoos 2, 114
teenager 34, 69, 74
testicles 102, 136, 163
testosterone 97pp., 101pp., 131
Texas 169
TG Forum 30
TGSF(Transgender San Francisco) 21, 25
thailand 137p.
thermolysis 118
thrift stores 17
toilet 57, 115, 145
Tootsie(movie) 10
toys 45p., 49
trachea 139
trannie 24p., 30, 35p., 44p., 63, 121
transdermal patch 98
transmissible yeast infection 147
Transsexual Women's Resources 31
triadic therapy 89
TS Roadmap 31
tuck,tucking 53, 81, 124
two-step SRS procedure 144, 148

U

unemployment 103, 110
unisex restroom 115
Unitarian(church) 26
United Airlines 28
Unity(church) 26
urethra 136, 144p., 147
urination 136, 143, 145, 147, 150

V

vaginoplasty 136, 143
Victoria's Secret 18, 30
violence 155
voice 100p., 117, 122p., 141
voter registration 126
vulva 137, 147p., 163

W

Wal-Mart   17
warrior, weekend   109
water-based lubricant   160
weekend warrior   109
West, Sarah   28p.
width, vaginal   161p.
wigs   22, 34, 121pp.
win-win situation   58
womb   7

woodworking   167
wrinkles   140

Y

Yahoo   30, 122
yeast infection   147, 150, 164

Z

Zoloft   58

About the author

Since the turn of the century (the 21st century, that is!) Lannie Rose has been writing about her experiences transitioning from a life in which she thought she was a man and had a successful career in computer hardware engineering, to a new life in which she knows she is a woman and thinks she will become a technical writer. Ms. Rose's writings have appeared in the e-zine Transgender Forum (www.tgforum.com), an online magazine for the transgender community. Several of Ms. Roses's pieces were incorporated into the Dennis Johnston Award-winning play *The Naked I: Monologues from Beyond the Binary* by Tobias K. Davis. Ms. Rose lives in San Jose, California, with her calico cat, Cali. She (Lannie, not Cali) invites you to visit her personal Web site, www.elainerose.com, or write to her at lannierose@gmail.com.

Printed in the United Kingdom
by Lightning Source UK Ltd.
126528UK00001B/352/A